Let's Get Real...Estate!

Simple, Proven, Step-by-step Path to Success in Real Estate Investing

By Daniel Papes

To my wife Christina,
my partner in real estate and in life.

Let's Get Real...Estate!

Simple, Proven, Step-by-step Path to Success in Real Estate Investing

By Daniel Papes

Registration with Library of Congress
Copyright © 2019 by Daniel Papes

Printed in the United States of America

First Printing, 2019
Second Printing 2020

Table of Contents

Preface

Twenty years of experience in one book.

If you focused on a profession for twenty years, learning more with each passing day, how good would you be at that profession twenty years later compared to when you started? Obviously much better. You would be an expert. This is true of any profession including brain surgery, teaching, accounting, or marketing.

Now, what if that profession is one of the most lucrative you can engage in, like, say real estate investing? All the better! You could indeed make hundreds of thousands, even millions, of dollars as an expert in real estate investing.

I am writing this book for one purpose: to share the lessons I learned over the past two decades of investing in real estate and to accelerate your understanding of this exciting and lucrative business. The hope is that you can follow in my footsteps except without having to invest twenty years to gain the experience.

You will see that I have had great success in investing in residential real estate, in aggregate making millions. But you will also see that I made some mistakes along the way, and learned some hard lessons that, at the time, cost me money. There is much to learn from my success, but there is an equal amount to learn from my mistakes. Given that I have done so well over the years, despite some errors, if you replicate what I did well, and avoid the errors I made, I'm sure you will experience similar great results, and much more quickly than I did!

The first chapter outlines what I call "The Ideal Scenario," which describes the perfectly executed real estate transaction from purchase to sale. Have I ever achieved one of these, and will you? No, I haven't, and likely neither will you. But doing most of the things in The Ideal Scenario well on a real estate transaction usually results in significant profits. Understanding what perfect looks like will be a guide to getting most of it right and make you great money along the way.

Each of the following chapters outlines a stage of a real estate transaction from evaluating properties and purchasing all the way to cashing out of your investment. I provide advice, real examples of great moves that I have made, and real examples of mistakes that I regretted but still learned from.

By your investing a few hours in *Let's Get Real...Estate! Simple, Proven, Step-by-Step Path to Success in Real Estate Investing,* I hope to save you years of on-the-job learning. I trust it will be very helpful to you, and I wish you great success in your real estate endeavors.

Dan Papes
Mount Kisco, New York
July 2019

Chapter 1 – The Ideal Scenario
How to execute the perfect real estate transaction

As you follow the methodologies I describe in this book, you will encounter my insights on various elements of residential real estate investments. These have all been developed based on my real-life experiences and, therefore, you know that they are more than theories. Thus, the dual meaning of the word "Real" in the title. Please keep in mind that the intention here is for you to learn from my experiences, both positive and negative, to increase your odds of success and level of profitability.

This short chapter defines for you what the ideal real estate investment scenario looks like. This is not a "what do we *expect* to achieve," but more "what are we *trying* to achieve" in order to maximize our success. This scenario describes the perfectly executed transaction, and if you execute it perfectly you will certainly earn a fantastic return. "Fantastic" returns may come on occasion, but "great" returns are, well, **great!** View this model as something to strive for and as a benchmark to guide your actions. I refer to each of the ideal scenario's elements throughout this book and provide you with advice to help you achieve objectives as close to ideal as possible.

Keep in mind the saying, "Close only counts with horseshoes and hand grenades." Well, they left out real estate investing when they made up this saying. "Close" to the Ideal Scenario equals positive cash flow and generous profits!

A word of warning here based on experience. DO NOT let the "perfect" become the enemy of "good enough.". In business, in life, and in real estate investing, you want to do well, you want to do the best you can, you want to succeed. But you do not need to be perfect. If you get close to most of the steps in the ideal scenario you will be successful. As you read through the steps, don't be intimidated and don't despair.

Here are the steps to reach that Ideal Scenario:

1. Buy Low! If you purchase your properties below market price you will have the security to know your assets have positive value immediately. Target 10% to 15% below market value for your purchase price. As a result, even before any appreciation

you will be ahead of the game.

2. Lease your property right away! Plan ahead when you are in the process of acquiring a property and get that first tenant lined up to move in as close to your closing date as possible.

3. Find a great tenant! Check them out thoroughly, a relatively small amount of time will save you from much frustration and financial strain in the future.

4. Reduce your labor! Put much of the workload on your tenant.

5. Create positive cash flow! Ensure your lease rate is competitive and that it also covers your projected costs. Much of this analysis should be done as you are setting your target purchase price.

6. Finance your property with minimum costs! Procure a mortgage that keeps your monthly expenses to a minimum while protecting you from dramatic increased costs during your projected ownership period.

7. Keep that property occupied! When it's time for a new tenant, plan and line up that tenant for a move-in date within days of your existing tenant's departure.

8. Sell high! Get top dollar for your investment as you close out. You made money on the purchase, you made money while you owned the property, and now you will make money selling it.

As you read the rest of this book, I will note for you how these concepts play into your day-to-day decisions and when in the process you can leverage them.

Any real estate investment that hits on all eight of these points is a sure winner. And a real estate investment that hits on most of these points will be a winner as well. Keep these in mind as you move forward in your journey.

Chapter 2 – Time to Buy
Select that first property

Ideal Scenario Alert: Purchase the property for 10% to 15% less than market value.

You have decided you want to invest in real estate, and you are ready to begin. The first question you must answer is "What kind of property will I invest in?" My success has been achieved in single and two-family homes, and I recommend the same to those of you just getting started and to those who will be managing a real estate portfolio as a side business to your career. There are tens and hundreds of thousands of dollars to be made with such properties. In addition, the complexity associated with managing a real estate portfolio is minimized since you will be dealing with only one or two tenants per property. However, my concepts apply to all types of residential investment properties (as well as some commercial properties).

Before I go further, it is important to make a comment on purchasing properties ethically. When I speak of purchasing a property at below market price, I do not mean to say you should "steal" a property from a seller, or trick them into selling to you instead of selling to someone else. Instead, I mean finding motivated sellers who are anxious to sell their properties to solid buyers at prices that the sellers are willing to accept. As long as you are behaving ethically, you can feel comfortable being aggressive in your efforts and offers. If the deal doesn't work for the seller, they will simply turn down your offer. If, for some unusual reason, I get a sense that a seller is in an unhealthy financial position and desperate, and that they are making a bad decision selling to me, I would not engage in the transaction.

With all that said, one early consideration as you set out to find a property is whether to use a realtor, and if you do use a realtor, which one. For your first transaction, perhaps your first two, I strongly recommend you use a buyer's realtor (a realtor who represents your interests as the buyer) and one who is very familiar with the area where you are buying. I cover buying with and without a realtor in Chapter 3. For the remainder of this chapter, I explore transactions that do not include a realtor.

So, what ARE you looking for in prospective properties?

1. A one- or two-family home in your home town, or an adjacent town, preferably no further than 20 minutes from your residence.
2. The purchase price in the range of your down-payment budget assuming a 20% down payment. For example, if you have $20,000 in the bank, look at properties in the $100,000 to $150,000 range (remember you will not be buying for the asking price; you will negotiate that price down).
3. An underpriced house versus the market, and/or a motivated seller (more on this in Chapter 4).

And now that you know what you are looking for, how do you find it? The ideal methods include:

1. Search realtor.com, Zillow, Trulia, Craigslist, and realtor websites in your local area.
2. Call local real estate firms and without committing to use their services, ask if they have listings that meet your criteria as described in item 2 on the previous page. Remember, they want to sell properties they have listed!
3. Be aware of houses for sale as you drive to work and through local neighborhoods.
4. Look for more than one property. Ideally, you want to have two or three prospects in progress at the same time with an eye towards closing at least one of them.
5. If you see houses for rent using the above sources, and there's something that catches your interest, contact the owner or the realtor to determine if the owner would consider selling.

****
A Personal Example
One of my more profitable acquisitions, one that proved to be a successful 18-month turnaround, was a house that was listed for **rent, not for sale.** The owner wasn't sure if she wanted to sell the property or rent it, but in the end decided to list it for rent to see what rental rate she could get. Upon receiving my call, she immediately went from "rent mode" to "sell mode," and we wrapped up the transaction and in a matter of 45 days the property was mine at a price nearly 18% below market. I have found that about 40% of people attempting to rent their property are willing to consider selling instead.
Don't miss such opportunities!
****

At any given time, even in small towns, there are at least a handful of opportunities to purchase property below market value. Your job is to find them and to purchase them for a compelling price.

Summary
1. Starting with one- and two-family homes allows you to learn the business without too much complexity.
2. Using a realtor for your first transaction or two enables long-term success when you go out on your own without a realtor. Begin to apply the concepts in this book even with a buyer's realtor involved.
3. Asking an owner if their rental property is available for purchase may lead to a successful transaction. Don't be afraid to ask.
4. Engage in transactions ethically.

Chapter 3 – The Realtor
Choose carefully when buying and selling

There are several pitfalls you can avoid by having a realtor, and you will learn much from them as you go through your first few transactions. Observe them closely and absorb all you can from them about your market and its unique characteristics. One warning, though. Realtors make money closing sales transactions. In Chapter 4, I outline strategies that involve patience, self-discipline, and the ability to walk away from a transaction that does not meet the objectives you have set. Realtors don't operate by this way of thinking and, thus, may encourage you to accept a deal that is not optimal. Avoid this at all costs! You must feel good about the deal without rationalization or encouragement.

****

A Personal Example

In the late 1990s, I was interested in acquiring an investment property with an asking price of $385,000. After evaluating comparable properties and collaborating with my realtor, she encouraged me to make an offer of $362,000, and be willing to move up in price from there. I was fairly new to real estate, and had what was probably, at the time, an over-confidence in myself to read a buying situation (over-confidence is an affliction my brothers will tell you I've had all my life!). I decided to offer $325,000. My realtor was aghast, but she was obligated to make my offer. Their counter? $345,000, a full $17,000 less than her suggested offer, and $60,000 less than the asking price! In my counter, I split the difference and offered $335,000. They countered at $338.000. While I thought I might be able to bring them down to my $335,000 offer, I decided this was a fair deal. The transaction closed at $338,000 -- $47,000 below asking, or 8.7%, and $24,000 less than the "bottom" price the realtor had recommended. It was from transactions like this that I learned I was ready to buy real estate without representation.

****

When setting your target purchase price (at least 10% below market), information is your very good friend. The seller's realtor is an excellent source of information that will help you determine the mindset and needs of the seller, and the price that you believe can win and gain you instant equity (buying for less than market value).

Questions for the Seller's Realtor

1. How long has the house been on the market?
   a. This question is often a key to understanding the anxiety of the seller. If the average days on the market in your area is 30 days, and the target property has been on for 120 days, you more than likely have a seller who is willing to negotiate. However, there are anxious sellers with homes on the market for only 10 days, so the "time on the market" rule is not universal, but it is a key indicator.
2. Is the seller trying to close by a certain date?
   a. Here again is an opportunity to learn how incented the seller is. For example, the answer could be "they have purchased a new home and are moving 45 days from now." A seller such as this would be very anxious about carrying two mortgages and, therefore, would likely sell at a lower price to a qualified buyer.
3. Why is the person selling?
   a. Often there are key clues in the answer to this question. Answers could include a corporate relocation, the residing family member passed away, or it is part of an estate, a divorce, downsizing, or upsizing.
   b. If it is a lifestyle sale (e.g. the owners are retired and considering moving from their home in New York and purchasing a new home in Florida), you are less likely to have a hungry seller who is willing to negotiate because the sellers are not under any time pressure.
4. Does the seller have any unique needs or desires regarding the sale of their property?
   a. Sometimes a seller has a unique set of needs or desires regarding the sale of their property. Understanding these characteristics may provide valuable clues to getting a lower price.

****

A Personal Example

In purchasing a two-family home about ten years ago, I asked a realtor this very question about the unique needs of the seller. Her answer was "Well, there is an 82-year-old woman who has lived in one of the units for 18 years and she wants to stay for one more year, but her rent is

$1,200 per month. That is $300 below market value. The owner has grown close to this woman over time and would strongly prefer the buyer of the home allow the woman to stay for another 12 months at that low rate." First, I would never purchase a property and kick out an 82-year-old person. But now I knew something the seller wanted in the transaction that, as it turned out, no one else was aware of. I made an offer that was $35,000 lower than the asking price and lower than two other offers by $12,000. Despite my lower offer, the owner decided to sell to me because I included a commitment in the offer to let the woman remain in the apartment. I ended up with a great deal that more than made up for the $3,600 below market rent on the woman's unit. The woman got to stay, and after the year was up, she left as she had planned, and I was able to rent to a new tenant at the going market rate.

****

In asking the questions on the previous page, you can develop an educated assessment of the likelihood of the seller's willingness to negotiate lower than their asking price, and importantly, lower than market value.

The Double-Ended Deal

Another way to lower the asking price while working with a realtor is the "double-ended deal." After searching realtor.com, Zillow, local real estate listings, Craigslist, and speaking to local real estate offices, you have identified the homes you are interested in that are in your price range (or within 20% of your price range). Note who the selling realtor AND the real estate firm are for those properties and call them to discuss your interest as well as to have your questions answered.

Why note the selling real estate firm and specific realtor? Because you want that real estate firm AND the listing realtor from that firm to double-end the deal. This means the firm and realtor can earn the "listing commission" of approximately 3% AND the "selling commission" of 3%, making a total of 6% commission for them. (Note: Sometimes the commission is 5%, but, still, the "extra" doubles their commission!)

To explain further, in most real estate transactions, there are two real estate firms involved: the listing (seller) firm and its realtor, and the buyer's firm and realtor. You are going to avoid having two realtors involved by forgoing a realtor for yourself and using the seller's realtor only. By involving the same realtor for both the buyer and the seller, you double that realtor's commission, creating a major financial incentive for them to help you make a deal with the seller! **Do not underestimate the value of this incentive and the influence it can have over a deal.** The agent is representing the seller, but in order to close the deal and double their commission, they will work very hard on your behalf to get the deal done. In my experiences, this has saved me hundreds of thousands of dollars in the aggregate. Not only will the realtor be working hard for their commission, the owner of the real estate company or branch will be pushing their agent hard to earn that double commission. She earns her commission by making a deal, even if it means sacrificing on the purchase price to get a deal done!

> *Example: A realtor is selling a house for $270,000 with a 6% commission agreement. The selling price ends up being $250,000. There are generally two possible scenarios for the payout to the realtor:*
> 1. *The house sells to a buyer represented by a buyer's realtor. The real estate agent for the seller earns 3% commission, or $7,500. The buyer's realtor also earns 3%, or $7,500. OR,*
> 2. *The house sells to a buyer who is using the seller's realtor. The realtor, therefore, earns $15,000, double what they would have made otherwise!*

It is very important in the double-ended situation to consider that if you do not know the market well, you will need to be diligent and conservative in your evaluation of your offering price. After all, that person represents the seller and you won't have a realtor formally on your side helping you understand the market. Thus, you need to take the time to review the asking price and determine your target price based on other recent sales of similar properties in the area.

"Similar" means the same number of bedrooms, bathrooms, approximate square footage, lot size, desirability of neighborhood and community, and, of course the condition of the home.

Obviously, the seller herself factors into the transaction as well, and even despite a motivated realtor, some sellers are not that anxious to sell, or are obstinate and won't lower their price to an acceptable level. If this is the case, give it some effort and if you can't reach an agreement at an acceptable price to you, move on to the next transaction without regrets. Remember our key objective in this phase is to BUY LOW!

Summary

1. Probe the selling realtor to understand why an owner is selling, looking for clues that can help you determine how much money to offer for the property and how anxious the seller is.
2. Discuss with the realtor any unique aspects of the sale and try to uncover "non-financial" motivations of the buyer, like my Personal Example of the 82-year-old tenant.
3. Do not be shy about offering a markedly lower price than the asking price.
4. Create a "double-ended" deal for the selling realtor to incent closure at your price.

Chapter 4 – Buy Low
Win right from the beginning

Perhaps the most important determinant of your level of profit from a real estate transaction is how you handle the acquisition of the property in the first place. It's not different from buying a stock. If you buy a stock at $50/share and it rises to $100/share and you sell, you have doubled your money (profit = $50/share). But if you buy it at $80/share and sell at $100, you've made $20/share. You want to buy that stock as low as possible in order to maximize your profit, and you want to do the same thing with a real estate investment. I want you buying a property at $50, not $80, and selling that property for $100 or more.

Setting a Target Price

Setting a target price, and sticking with it, is critical. Without a target price you will find yourself wandering along an undefined continuum and you may not have the discipline to know when to walk away from what would be an unprofitable or, at least, a nonoptimized transaction.

Your target price should be set by two key factors:

1. The first and most important reference point is comparable home sales in the area. In real estate, the word "comparables" (or "comps") has several meanings, but your definition should be "sales of similar properties in the immediate vicinity in the last 24 months." Not "for sale" properties because anyone can set a price they want for a house they are selling and yet never sell for that amount. You want to know what people actually "paid" for properties similar to the one you are pursuing. Note that comparables are quite variable, and you should choose the most conservative (lowest price) comps you can find. Sites like Zillow and Trulia are useful only when they show properties actually "sold," not "Zestimates" which are often inaccurate. You should use estimates in your negotiation if they are lower than your target price (see later in this chapter) but disregard them if they are higher.

2. The second factor to consider is what your cash flow will be if you acquired the property and rented it to a tenant. Assuming you will have a mortgage, you should calculate the mortgage (less the down payment), taxes, and insurance payment you

13

will incur if you purchase the property at the target price. This tells you your monthly cost for the property, which gives you half the picture. The next number you need is your likely rental income. This is more difficult to calculate because there is not an extensive record available as to what properties have rented for. It is here you must rely on current rental listings for similar properties. Since you are not relying on "rented" data, but on "for rent" data, you need to do a bit of homework. Visit a few of the competitive properties, feel out the owner on what the final rental price would be, and gauge for yourself what the market rental price is for your apartments or house. After all, it's the rentals in your area that you will be competing with, and you want your value to your tenants to be equal to or better than theirs.

To summarize, you need the following in order to estimate your cash flow:
1. Comparable "sold" prices in your target area.
2. Monthly mortgage cost.
3. Monthly insurance cost.
4. Monthly local tax cost.
5. Estimated rental income based on comparables.

With the acquisition and cash flow information in hand, and a solid idea of what the likely rent will be, you can build an equation that suits your situation. For instance, you may need at least break-even cash flow, you may need positive cash flow (proceed with caution if you are in this category), or you may be able to live with negative cash flow if (because of rental property deductions, such as interest expense and depreciation) you can afford to carry the property and generate profit after tax. Whatever your situation, be conservative, prepare for a potential gap in tenants (a period when one lease expires and a new tenant has not moved in), or a late payment or two, so that you don't get caught in a cash squeeze.

Ideal Scenario Alert: The monthly lease rate equals your expenses plus at least 5%.

The breakdown of monthly costs on the next page gives you an idea of what a reasonable target price would be and whether you can generate the cash flow needed to sustain the property. (Keep in mind, by the way, that what is happening here is the tenant is "buying" your

14

property for you. They are paying the costs, but you are increasing your equity!).

Monthly mortgage cost	**$1,100**
Insurance	**$95**
Local taxes	**$200**
Common charges	**$100**
Total Costs	**$1,495**
Projected rental income	**$1,600**
Net Positive Cash Flow	**$105** (Remember that

after tax your profit should be markedly higher)

With the target price in hand, your first offer is going to be lower than the target to give you room to negotiate and potentially raise your offer without exceeding our target price.

My goal in any real estate purchase is to generate "instant equity," meaning that the day you buy the property it is worth more than you paid for it. Thus, if you had to, you could sell the property you just bought for equal to or more than you just paid. You will have reduced your monthly cash outflow and, most importantly, you have "built in" profit from day one.

> ➤ *Example: Let's look at a situation that I once faced when looking at a two-family home on the market for $250,000. By analyzing comparable sales, I determined that $240,000 was approximately the price this property would sell at in the then current market. I set a target price of $210,000, giving me $30,000 of "instant equity." In this situation, I began with an offer of $180,000, hoping to purchase at this price but giving me $30,000 in headroom ($180,000 versus the target price of $210,000) to negotiate with if needed.*

When I advise investors on this approach and explain the suggested initial offer price, they often cringe. They feel embarrassed to offer $180,000 for a property that is on the market for $250,000. But why not try $180,000 and see what the reaction is? The seller may reject it emotionally, or they may counter with $220,000. I've seen some amazing things in my experience where through low offers I get lower than my target price even right after my first offer.

A Personal Example
A property owner listed their house for $310,000. I offered $240,000.
He countered with $260,000. Surprise!
This person is more anxious to sell than I thought!

It is more likely, however, that you will have multiple iterations with this strategy. You will offer $240,000 and the seller may not even respond or may counter with $290,000. Either way, you are still in the game and the negotiations are on. If you don't get emotional you are on a potential path to success. Closely observe the situation, see what your shared realtor is saying about the buyer's reaction, listen to her choice of words carefully, and even take notice of the body language she is conveying to you. Remember, that realtor wants to get a deal done and earn that double commission (See the Double-Ended Deal, Chapter 3).

Negotiation on this opportunity continues, but because my methodology involves potential rejection some number of times before getting a deal, it is a good idea to have another transaction or two in the pipeline. This helps you be less emotional on any one of them, knowing if one fails, you have others to pursuit.

In the case above, I acquired the property for $250,000!

Testing Your Target Offer with Pre-Renting
Since the entry price to your real estate investment is so critical to your success, you may want to use a methodology that I have deployed in the past I call "pre-renting." Pre-renting allows you to do a reasonably accurate assessment of the property you are about to acquire and to do so in three easy steps.

1. The first step with pre-renting is to look at Craigslist and other real estate internet sites to determine what comparable properties are asking for in rent. Do these rates match with what you have in your planning calculations? Are you being too optimistic, or too conservative? These comparables will help you gain a better perspective on this.
2. The second step in pre-renting is to place a "for rent" ad on Craigslist for the property you are about to purchase. List all its features, even use photos, and describe it as precisely as possible. If you receive a lot of calls and emails, you know you are in the ballpark. If your phone is silent and your inbox

empty, your price is likely too high. It's important to note that if you do receive lots of calls you may have priced your rent too low, so try to fine tune your ad to get an accurate reading on the highest possible rent you can reasonably command.

3. The third step is an extension of the second. If you can execute the timing effectively it would make for a great transaction. Assume for a minute you put an ad out for the rental of a property at a price that fits well with your financial objectives. In such a case, you may be able to capture that tenant and aggressively close on the property at the same time. You can have a signed lease in hand even before closing on the property! You would not have any lag in rental income from closing to occupancy, improving your cash flow in a meaningful way by saving you one to three months of vacancy when you are paying a mortgage but don't have any rental income to offset it.

Avoid Emotion

Do not become emotionally wrapped up in a deal. I have done so before, and it resulted in my paying too high a price or lingering too long on a transaction that never came to fruition. As effective buyers, we need to keep in mind that there is always another transaction; there are always good values and we just need to look for them and not worry about the ones that didn't close. I cannot emphasize enough that emotion is arguably the biggest obstacle you will encounter as you endeavor to make a profit in real estate investing.

Often emotion manifests in your ego or pride. As you examine properties and engage in making offers and counter offers, you will often be tempted to "win." Winning based on a prideful negotiation versus a prudent and disciplined negotiation can be quite expensive. Think of "winning" as purchasing a home at or below your target price, not as just having your offer accepted.

Another emotional hazard is rationalization. I have found myself beginning a negotiation with a seller based on what I think is the highest reasonable price for a property. As the negotiation proceeds, and the sellers come back with their best and final counter offer, which is above my target price. It is at this point that rationalization can kick in! I might find myself saying "Well, maybe I was too conservative in setting my target price, perhaps this property is actually worth more than I originally thought." When this happens, beware! Occasionally you may be correct and your target price was too conservative, but more often you were correct in setting your target price and you should stick to it. Keep in mind it is definitely better to walk away from deals when you suspect that your target prices may have been too conservative then to over pay for a property that creates cash flow problems, or that you lose money on when you go to sell it.

Note, too, that emotion plays a part in other ways. Many real estate investors are undone by choosing a realtor based on emotion versus the realtor's professional success, by renting to tenants based on affability versus an established historical ability to pay their rent on time, and by modifying lease terms that are against your interests.

The counters to emotion are: Data, facts, history, empirical information, comparable historical sales and rental data, input from unbiased realtors and other experts, and, in my case, my spouse!

****

A Personal "Don't" Example

I was looking at a luxury condominium in a new development where construction wasn't even completed. It was a unique property with no reasonable comparables. In such a case as this, the market would set the price in the first several transactions but hadn't done so yet because the property was so new. The purchase price SEEMED reasonable, but I did not know and had little data for comparison. For several days, I stewed over this potential purchase, and on one particular visit (and caught in the path of a phenomenal salesperson!) I found myself sitting inside a beautiful model suite and made the decision to buy. Sure enough, after six months the market defined itself and settled at about 10% below what I had paid --"instant negative equity," something you want to avoid. My mistake was caused by emotion. I saw the beauty of the suite, imagined the potential for the property, and I took the unfortunate leap. On the bright side, this property rented with positive cash flow well above the expenses, but had I waited six months I could have had that great rental income on a 10% lower cost base.

****

The Offer Price: Plenty of Fish in the Sea

I will share a true story that illustrated a key concept for purchasing investment real estate. When I was in college, my friend and I would go to Spring Break at Daytona Beach with the primary objective to meet college women who were also on their Break. I was always the shy one and timid about approaching someone at the many clubs in Daytona. My good friend, Matt, on the other hand, had no such trepidation. If he saw a woman who caught his interest, he simply walked up to her, introduced himself, and started a conversation. This strategy would fail four times out of five. But on the fifth time, he had himself a date. When I asked him about the rejections, he simply said that you can't worry about the rejections, just know that somewhere along the way there would be an acceptance. For him, there was no loss in having tried the first four and failed because the fifth one allowed him to forget the others. His comment to me, insensitive though it may be, was: "There are plenty of fish in the sea."

While I could never execute Matt's strategy at Daytona Beach, I use it effectively all the time in real estate. I look for property to purchase, I set a goal for acquisition cost, I make offers (see Chapter 6) and if I do not get my goal price, I move on to the next. No harm is done having tried; I may have learned a few things along the way and I continue in my pursuit of that "fifth" property!

You will find that over time your success rate in finding properties will improve. As you gain experience you will more quickly dismiss properties that are an unlikely fit, and recognize properties that have high odds of being successful. As you build this experience you will become more efficient, your investments will be more lucrative both during your ownership period and when it comes time to sell. It is really like most things in life, the more time and experience you get at reviewing properties the better you will become at it!

The "Free Living" Scenario

While I have never taken the opportunity to "live free," the concept is to purchase a two-family or four-family house and as the owner of property   live in one of the units yourself, and have your costs partially or fully covered by the tenants in the other units.

Living in one of the units in a multi-family situation can work well for an inexperienced investor who wants to try a few real estate acquisitions but does not want to take excessive risks. One needs a place to live anyway and, thus, when you as the investor is your own tenant the financial risk is reduced. This arrangement can also work well for younger people, perhaps someone single or a young couple. If you have a family it becomes somewhat more complex as a larger unit is needed, and you may not want to expose your children to tenants living in such close proximately. While you should do some level of background check on your tenants, you simply never know who you are going to end up with, so best to be cautious if you have a family.

I have owned multi-family properties where the "live in one of the units" scenario would have worked although in the end I decided to rent out both. I purchased a two-family house in a and rented each unit for $3,000 for a total rental income of $72,000 a year per month. The costs to carry the house were approximately $14,000 per. Had I rented only one unit and retained the other unit for me I still would have had a healthy positive cash flow and profit, nearly $22,000! While that was an unusually profitable situation, there are often scenarios where you can own a multi-family property and have the rental income from the other units cover all your expenses as the investor living in the other unit. This is free living!

Summary
1. The purchase price becomes the foundation of your profit opportunity in the future.
2. Set a target price and stick to it.
3. Calculate your cash flow thoughtfully.
4. Pre-rent for price validation and uninterrupted cash flow.
5. Do not shy away from making offers much lower than the asking price.
6. There are plenty of fish in the sea, keep your emotions at bay.
7. In your early investment experiences consider using one of the units of a multi-family property your own residence.

Chapter 5 – Financial Analysis
Calculating potential and real return on investments

There are several common and effective ways to analyze potential and real returns on residential real estate investments. In this chapter, I will review a few of the calculations that I like to use when I am considering investing in a property. Most commercial real estate companies use versions of these equations to compare different investment options, and their analyses are extremely detailed. For your purposes, I recommend you become familiar with these equations, but use them as guides to create valuable inputs into your decision-making process.

Before I go further, I want to note that, for me, the most valuable investment considerations are that:

1. Is it a quality property in a quality neighborhood?
2. Is the property low maintenance, or one that will become low maintenance with upgrades?
3. Does the property have a positive cash flow?
4. Is there a strong opportunity for appreciation (most often a result of item one above)?

That said, let's explore some of the more common calculations in the residential real estate business.

Net Operating Income (NOI)
This calculation is helpful to you and the bank that may be providing financing for your real estate investments. The NOI calculates the "operating revenue" of a real estate asset and becomes a key input into the Capitalization Rate and the Return on Investment (both covered later in this chapter). The NOI is determined as follows:

Rental Income – Operating Expenses = NOI

Operating expenses include those that you as the landlord are responsible for, including insurance, utilities (if they aren't the tenant's responsibility), anticipated repairs/maintenance, homeowner's association fees, local taxes, and the like. It does not include mortgage payments or capital expenditures. Here is an example for a property:

Rental rate	**$3,000** per month/**$36,000** per year
Insurance	**$1,000 per year**
Local taxes	**$4,000** per year
Utilities and repairs	**$3,000** per year
NOI	**$36,000 - $8,000**, or **$28,000**

Capitalization Rate ("Cap Rate")

The capitalization rate of a real estate investment tells you what the ROI on your investment is in an "all-cash" scenario. When considering an asking price or determining your target price for a property, the Cap Rate can be very handy. Cap Rate is determined as follows:

Cap Rate = NOI ÷ Purchase Price

Let's continue the example from above, which revealed a $28,000 NOI. If the asking price of a property is $300,000, and you paid the asking price, the Cap Rate is 9.3% ($28,000 ÷ $300,000).

To take this example further, let's assume you use the Cap Rate as a key input into setting your target price, and you want to invest only in properties that have a Cap Rate of 10% or higher. As such, you would set your target price at $280,000 for this property ($28,000 ÷ $280,000 = 10%).

While there are many factors that should influence your interest in a property and the value of your investment, I like to have a Cap Rate of 7% or higher when possible.

Return on Investment (ROI)

While this is arguably the most valuable calculation you can do on a prospective real estate investment, it is also the most difficult to accurately estimate. The ROI is determined as follows:

ROI = Gain on Investment - Cost of Investment ÷ Cost of Investment

The reason this is difficult to calculate in advance of buying a property is that you will need to make several key assumptions, including total rental income, appreciation of the property, maintenance costs, vacancy periods, tax rates and increases, and more. This does not mean that you should not do an ROI analysis, but keep in mind that it is based on assumptions and, therefore, should be taken as an estimate.

I find it helpful to run multiple ROI scenarios, assuming more conservative and more liberal levels of appreciation, the impact of an unexpected expense or vacancy, and other potential factors.

Continuing our example above and extending it into an ROI calculation, let's assume the following:

Purchase price	**$280,000**
Acquisition and sale costs	**$20,000**
Maintenance, insurance, interest, taxes, and other expenses	
	$30,000
Rental income	**$144,000**
Sale Price	**$325,000**

Your costs are $330,000 ($280,000 + $20,000 + $30,000) and your income is $469,000 ($325,000 + $144,000).

The ROI equation looks like this:
Your Gain on Investment – Cost of Investment = $139,000 ($469,000 - $330,000) ÷ your Cost on Investment ($330,000).

The ROI is, therefore, 42%. Assuming a reasonable holding period (6 years or less), this property would be an investment well worth making.

There are other equations to take into account when looking at real estate investing, including Internal Rate of Return (IRR), Return on Invested Capital (ROIC), and Payback. I would just advise against developing "analysis paralysis" and simply execute a cash-flow analysis and use the equations covered in this chapter.

Summary:
1. There are financial equations and analyses that you can leverage to ensure you are making a good investment – a quality property at a fair price in a high-demand neighborhood.
2. Net Operating Income, or NOI, gives you a clear view of the revenue you will generate from a particular investment.

3. Capitalization Rate, or Cap Rate, gives you a view of the return on an investment without financing costs. Typically, being in double digits (>10%) makes a property a good investment.
4. Return on Investment, or ROI, provides a comprehensive view of the percentage return you will make during an assumed holding period for a real estate asset.

Chapter 6 – Terms of the Offer
Creativity wins the day

An often-overlooked tool for winning in real estate is the written offer you make to a seller, and its terms. Leveraging terms has allowed me to buy at least four properties that I would not have won otherwise, making me hundreds of thousands of dollars in the process. An astute seller (or one with a quality realtor) knows the value of certain offer terms; sometimes the offer terms can trump a higher priced offer from another buyer and allow you to acquire the property for a lower price. As stated in Chapter 3, spend plenty of quality time with your realtor to understand the motivations of the seller and what they may value beyond the selling price.

What might motivate a seller beyond price? You won't know until you ask, and ask you should. Here are some terms I have found meaningful to sellers:

1. Cash Sale. One of the biggest risks a seller faces is the failure of a buyer to secure their mortgage. Offering to pay cash, and providing evidence that you have that cash, allows the seller to remove the most important contingency in a real estate sale: the mortgage contingency. Mortgages take approximately two and half to four months to complete and can result in a bank rejection late in the process, leaving a seller hanging for months and then losing the sale. Now they need to start the process all over again! When I am selling, I am willing to take 5% less in purchase price, maybe more, to remove a mortgage contingency and make a cash sale. Let me illustrate.

➢ *Example: You are the seller of a property for $400,000. You receive two offers that arrive on the same day, March 1. One is from John who offers your full purchase price but with a mortgage contingency. The second offer is from Mary for $392,000 cash with no mortgage contingency. In Scenario One, you make a "price only" decision and accept the higher price of $400,000. John signs the contract and then diligently applies for a mortgage, a process that takes at least two weeks to get started as he needs to provide the bank with mounds of data. By March 15, the bank has all they need, and they begin their review* *of John's finances. On June 1, the bank informs John that, unfortunately, he does not qualify for the mortgage and they must reject his application. You, as the seller, have now lost three months and must start all over to find a new buyer. Worse, Mary thought she lost the opportunity to purchase your property and has since purchased a different property. It could be many months before you find another buyer and may have to go through the mortgage delay once again. You could lose six months or even as long as a year before you find a replacement buyer. Scenario One was a disaster for you and you wonder if that $8,000 offer difference was worth it! In Scenario Two, if you had decided to accept Mary's "cash offer" with no mortgage contingency, the title search and property inspection are completed, certified checks are received, and you close your sale on March 15. This example reveals the power of an all cash offer!*

2.   Remove the "mortgage contingency" from the purchase contract. Most buyers sign a contract that only comes into full effect once their mortgage has been approved by a bank. In other words, the mortgage is contingent upon the bank approval. If you do not have the cash to purchase the house outright, but you are 99% sure that you will qualify for the mortgage you can state in your offer letter that you have "no mortgage contingency." In doing so, you generate similar benefits to that of a "cash sale" in that the seller has the confidence that she will not lose the sale due to a mortgage rejection. The mortgage process can delay the sale for 60 days or longer, but the seller knows that she won't be 90 days down the road only to find you were rejected for the mortgage.

3.   Prequalification Letter. Offers that contain a bank's "pre-qualification letter" are viewed as stronger than those that do not. The "prequal" letter from the bank essentially says that you appear to qualify for a mortgage at a level required to purchase the property. Many sellers value this document, though it is non-binding. Personally, I do not give a pre-qualification letter much weight when I am selling a property as they are very easy to get from financial institutions because they are loaded with disclaimers. However, sellers tend to see you as a stronger buyer than buyers with no such

prequalification letter.

4. Inspection Waiver. Most purchase contracts contain an "inspection contingency," meaning that if you sign the contract you are committed to purchase the property unless your engineer's inspection shows an issue that was not disclosed by the seller (e.g. termite damage or a leaky roof). Most owners are notoriously insecure about the condition of their home and are almost always concerned the inspection will reveal the many problems their house has accumulated over the years (in most cases these concerns are ill-placed as, we tend to be more critical of our own homes than we should be). Waiving the inspection ensures the seller that a week after the offer is accepted you will not come to them with a list of issues that need remediation, which cost time and money. Waiving the contingency also allows the acquisition process to start and end sooner which most savvy sellers value greatly. However, there is a way to eliminate all the risk associated with waiving the inspection. Simply have an engineer execute the inspection between the time you have an "accepted offer" and when the contract is signed. It usually takes five to six business days after an offer is accepted to get the purchase contract done and you can use this time to have your inspector thoroughly examine the property and identify any issues that may need to be remediated.

➤ *Example: John and Joan each make offers to purchase a $200,000 property for the same price, $190,000. The seller was hoping to sell for $188,000 or more so both offers meet his threshold. However, John's offer contains an inspection contingency while Mary's does not. All other terms and conditions offered by these potential buyers are the same. The seller sees value in the inspection waiver and, therefore, decides, smartly, to choose Mary's offer over John's.*

Now that her offer has been accepted, Mary can take three different paths forward regarding an inspection.

Path One: Two days after acceptance of her offer, she has her inspector/engineer fully examine the property. The inspectors find no issues so Mary proceeds with the purchase process, the first step of which is signing the contract when it is ready three days later.

Path Two: The inspector finds a few issues that add up to a relatively small mitigation cost of $1,500. Mary knows she has plenty of "instant equity" based on her purchased price, and decides to proceed with the purchase at the offered price, signing the contract three days later.

Path Three: The inspector finds significant termite damage and estimates mitigation costs at $15,000. In this case, Mary either walks away from the purchase (keep in mind she has not signed a contract yet, she has simply made a non-binding offer) or she requests that the seller reduce the price by $15,000. Mary could also request that the seller fix the termite damage at their expense. If the seller will not do either of these, Mary can walk from the transaction and allow the seller to negotiate a deal with someone else. It is also interesting to consider this from the seller's side. If you were selling a property and an inspection revealed termite damage and you were not willing to remediate it in some way (price reduction or repair the damage), you are likely avoiding a problem that will arise once again with the next buyer. It is in the seller's best interest to either fix the termite damage or negotiate the price with the buyer they have in hand, in this case, Mary.

5. Bidding to win. Sometimes there are desirable property investments with multiple interested buyers who make offers, creating a competitive situation. When this happens, you can offer an all-cash purchase price, remove the mortgage contingency, or waive the inspection, in order to make your offer stand out. But there is another method that I used to acquire one of my most prized properties. I call it "the eBay" method because, like bidding on eBay, my offer automatically increases if I am outbid.

****

A Personal Example

There was a prized property on the market and, knowing there would be multiple offers, the seller's realtor requested all bids be submitted by 6 P.M. on the following Friday. The asking price was $500,000 and my target price was $525,000 (a unique situation where there was $100,000 to $200,000 more value after modest renovations). I submitted a $500,000 bid but with an additional statement: "My offer price is $500,000, but if there is a higher bid, I will match that bid plus $5,000, not to exceed a total purchase price of $525,000." As it turned out, the highest competitive offer was $512,000, which "automatically" made my offer $517,000. My offer was thereby the highest by $5,000 and I won the bid and the property. This particular investment turned into an amazing success, making more than $200,000 in profit. Any offer over $500,000 and under $520,000 made me the winner. I protected myself on the upside by putting a "not to exceed" clause that limited my exposure to my target price of $525,000. (Note: I also used my waiver of mortgage and inspection contingencies on this situation as well.)

****

6. Market Timing. Every market has a better and a worse season to buy and sell. Better selling seasons generate higher prices (bad for buyers, good for sellers) and worse selling seasons generate lower average prices (good for buyers, bad for sellers). As a buyer and seller, you should make yourself aware of these seasons in order to maximize your profits. Said another way, use seasons to "buy low and sell high!" For example, the Southwest Florida "snowbird" season is November through April. This is when northerners descend on Florida and their second homes to avoid harsh winter weather. If you want to acquire a house in Florida, know that sellers view the snowbird season as the optimal time to sell and, therefore. tend to put their homes on the market just before or early in the snowbird season. If you are a buyer you will pay more during this season, perhaps well more, than if you were willing to wait until the end of the season.

Consider this from a seller's perspective. In November, they know the market will be flooded with buyers and are highly optimistic about their ability to sell. They price their property aggressively high, but still within reason for market conditions. They are much more likely to find a buyer and sell their property at a satisfactory price than they would late in the season or in the off season. (When is it cheaper to buy a short-sleeved shirt in New York, in June or September?) However, if the seller prices their property too high, does not put it on the market until late in the season, or puts it on the market in the off season, in all likelihood the seller will encounter a difficult situation. They could find themselves in mid-May, the end of the season, without having sold their house. The population in their Florida city has halved as the snowbirds have returned home and, in the best case, they are likely staring at carrying their house at least until the following November. The options in such a situation are to accept a low-priced offer in the off season, or wait until November to put the house on the market again when the flood of buyers return.

> *Example: A house in a golf-course community was on the market for $410,000 in November. Several potential buyers visited the home but only one made an offer, $360,000, in mid-December, which the seller rejected. Why? Because the seller thought the house was worth $400,000, and it was mid-season, and they had plenty of time to find another buyer. In April, the house was still on the market and the seller was discouraged. She lamented turning down the $360,000 offer. During the entire season, people had looked at her home and decided it was not worth the price she was asking. On June 1, with the season well over, a buyer makes an offer of $340,000. Fearing a long holding period in the off-season, the seller accepts the offer and the transaction executes at that price. This is a good deal for the buyer and a disappointing but begrudgingly acceptable deal for the seller.*

Summary
1. Use offer terms to acquire properties at lower prices and to defeat competing offers.
2. Understand a seller's motivations. There is often hidden opportunity if you do!
3. Use the "eBay method" in competitive bids in order not to be outbid. Protect yourself on the upside with a "not to exceed" clause.
4. Understand that a "cash sale" is extremely valuable to a seller and should allow you to buy at a lower price and win in competitive bidding situations.
5. Eliminate the mortgage contingency to make a purchase offer much more valuable and save the seller considerable time and risk.

6. Waive the inspection contingency to add value to the seller and still be able to protect yourself with a quick inspection prior to contract signing.
7. Be aware of "seasonality" in your market -- buy in slow periods and sell in high-demand periods in order to maximize profits.

Chapter 7 – Financing
Mortgage, cash flow, and profit

Ideal Scenario Alert: Pay the lowest monthly payment possible without exposing yourself to dramatic increases in rates during the period you own the property.

While the purchase price is the number one critical success factor in real estate investing, how you choose to finance the property can make a significant difference in your cash flow and profitability. The path you choose could ensure cash flow comfort or condemn you to the dread of the first day of every month when your mortgage payment is due. Choose carefully.

It is important to know that I am not a financial advisor nor am I a certified expert in tax matters. You should consult your tax or financial advisor to confirm your chosen approach or to review your options. I am simply sharing with you mortgage structures that I have used or contemplated and that have worked effectively for me. I am also sharing the lessons I have learned over time.

Let's start with where to get your mortgage. Many people choose to procure their mortgage from the bank where they have their personal accounts. This is almost always a mistake! An individual bank has only a limited number of options and rates available to you. It is highly unlikely that if you look at only one bank (your current bank) you will find the optimal financing situation for your needs.

As such, I strongly suggest that you use a mortgage broker to help you find the best rates and to expose you to the maximum number of financing alternatives. It is nearly impossible for a non-professional to navigate the plethora of options in the marketplace and a broker can help you do this. Fees for the broker are almost always paid by the financial institution so there is no incremental cost to you when taking advantage of a broker's expertise! If for some reason you decide not to use a mortgage broker, be sure to do a broad survey of banks to determine which institution has the most advantageous interest rates and structures to meet your needs. Rates vary widely between different banks!

What follows is my philosophy on down payments and interest

rates and a review of several of the mortgage structures that I have used or been exposed to over time. Leveraging my experiences and advice should save you years of learning and hopefully large sums of money in aggregate. (See Appendix A page TK for details on mortgage types.)

Most financial advisors consider it a bad financial habit to own an asset without equity in that asset and I agree with them. The larger your down payment, the more equity you have. If you have a solid equity foundation and need to sell the asset for some reason, you will not find yourself "underwater," or owing more on the loan than you can sell the asset for. HOWEVER, if you follow my methodology in Chapters 1 and 2, you will have "instant equity" based on the low price you paid. For instance, if you buy a property for $200,000 but that property is worth $250,000, you have $50,000 in equity right out of the gate. This equity can provide the same benefit as a $50,000 down payment. As such, you can feel comfortable making the smallest down payment the mortgage provider will allow and still provide you the desired mortgage. The philosophy here is "buy well and minimize your down payment." Mortgage debt is the cheapest debt you can get and, therefore, it is to your benefit to borrow as much as possible (versus using your own cash for the down payment).

Mortgage Interest: Cheap Debt

For many people, mortgage debt is likely the cheapest debt they can find. If you itemize on your tax returns, odds are that you can deduct your mortgage interest payments and, thereby, realize a reduction in debt at your marginal tax rate.

That's a lot to absorb so let me illustrate:

If you pay $10,000 in interest for your investment property in a given year, here is a basic view of the tax implications:

Mortgage interest paid in a given year	**$10,000**
Mortgage interest rate	**4%**
Marginal tax rate	**25%**
After tax, interest rate (assuming you itemize)	**3%**
After tax interest expense	**$7,500**

It is difficult to find better after-tax interest rates than this, especially when you compare mortgage rates to those of personal loan rates and credit card interest rates. (Note: Consolidating debt into a mortgage or home equity loan can sometimes be a great idea. Please consult your tax advisor).

Now that we know that mortgage debt is some of the best debt you can have, let's explore a few different options for mortgage structures. There are literally hundreds of structures one can select from, but I have chosen to describe loans that I have used or considered using in the past. Hopefully my comments will help you effectively make decisions on your investment mortgages.

Option 1; The 30-year fixed-rate mortgage

While one can be dazzled by many mortgage options, the 30-year fixed rate is the safest and most traditional model. Payments are fixed at the same amount for 30 years and, as a result, over time your payments become more and more manageable (cash flow turns more positive) as rental rates increase with inflation and your monthly payments remain the same. There are mortgages that generate lower monthly payments, but often you are sacrificing short-term gains for longer-term risk. In each investment situation, you must assess that risk as you consider your options.

Option 2: The 15-year fixed-rate mortgage

For the disciplined real estate investor, I see no reason to use this vehicle. If you do not want to take on the 30-year obligation, and prefer something shorter, simply procure a 30-year mortgage and make additional principle payments each month. A 15-year mortgage creates a commitment to a higher monthly payment and, in times of vacancy or personal financial strain, why constrain yourself to such a thing? You can pay off your 30-year mortgage in 15 years if you like, but you cannot pay off your 15-year mortgage in 30 years. Avoid this option.

Option 3: 5/1 Year Adjustable Rate Mortgage (ARM)

There are many versions of ARMs with different terms, but my concepts can be applied across most. In a 5/1, your rate remains fixed for 5 years, then can adjust every year after that depending on a financial index, such as the Prime Rate (set by the Federal Reserve). Usually the rate for the first 5 years is a "teaser" rate that is lower than the market rate, but in subsequent years your mortgage rate can increase as much as 2% a year up to 6% in total (there are many other versions, but this is typical). Thus, a 3% mortgage rate can become 9% in as few as 8 years into your mortgage. Yikes! This is, of course, a worst-case scenario, but it is possible and something that can realistically happen.

It is important to note that the longer the initial period, the further out your risk is pushed. For instance, on a 7/1 ARM, you have 7 years before you experience a potential rate increase. In the event you plan to hold the property for less than 7 years, you could benefit from the teaser rate during the entire period you own the property. However, be forewarned, often "planned" holding periods can be prolonged given poor market conditions or other unforeseen issues (including a profitable property that you don't want to sell after all), so plan conservatively and if anything, overestimate your holding period if you decide to use an ARM.

Option 4: Interest Only 30-year Adjustable Rate Mortgage (7/1)
This is a recent discovery of mine and I really like it, though it takes discipline to manage it effectively so ensure that you are prepared to exercise such discipline.

With an interest only 7/1 (or it could be a 5/1, or a 10/1), you pay the interest only on the amount borrowed for 7 years, then the loan is amortized over the remaining 23 years; payments after the initial 7 years include principle. The opportunity here is to have lower payments in the initial period of the loan. You do risk the payment going up significantly at the end of that initial period (remember, your principle is amortized over 23 years, packing more principle obligation into a shorter period) but also consider that rental rates typically increase over time as well so you may be collecting more rent in the later years.

However, I do not recommend this loan structure unless you are willing to do one of two very important things:

1. Sell the house well within the 7-year period. In such a case, you will have had the lowest possible monthly cash outflow, a market rate rental income, and never be exposed to the additional principle payment that kicks in after year 7.
2. Pay down the principle during the initial 7-year period. This loan works very well for someone like me, who some months wants to pay interest only, and in other months wants to make a meaningful payment to reduce the principle obligation.

****
A Personal Example
Today I have a 7/1 interest-only mortgage on a $270,000 loan. In the first 3 years, I have paid down the principle to $205,000, and I expect that at the end of the 7 years (if I still own the property) I will owe about $140,000 in principle. When the principle payment is factored into the 23-year remaining period, I will have a much smaller amount

to pay off. When you compare this to a 30-year fixed-rate mortgage, my overall payments will be much lower than 7/1 interest-only loan.

****

Let's compare the 7/1 Interest-Only Mortgage to a 30-year Fixed-Rate Mortgage based on a $250,000 Mortgage:

30-year Fixed-Rate payment at 4.5% interest

	$1,266/month
7/1 Interest-Only payment	**$937/month**
Cash flow difference	**$329/month**
Annual cash flow difference	**$3,948**

My experience is that planned holding periods (period from purchase to sale) for investment real estate can change. Sometimes this is voluntary (I decide I want to hold on to the property longer than I originally planned, or to sell sooner) and sometime involuntary (the market is in a slump; thus, demand and prices are low, and I choose not to sell in that market. Selling in a slump damages profits!)

It is especially the latter situation that you want to plan for. If you finance property on a 5/1 ARM, and plan on selling it within 5 years, and the market slumps, you could get stuck with increasing payment obligations and an inability to sell. This could create a challenging cash flow situation for you as your monthly expenses rise but your rental income stays flat. Plan conservatively, or at least, assess your ability to cover a "worst case scenario" in the event it arises. This is prudent investment real estate discipline.

About "Points"

Some mortgages have "points," a term describing a fee that you, the borrower, pays to the bank for a specific mortgage in exchange for a reduced interest rate. One point usually means 1% of the purchase price, which could be a substantial sum. Typically, the interest rate reduction generated by paying points has a longer payback than your typical investment property holding period, and it also requires an up-front payment that you would rather not make. I have never paid points and I suggest that you do not either. It is rare that I have kept a mortgage in place (without selling the property or refinancing) long enough to make paying points worth the reduced interest rate. Sticking to our philosophy of keeping expenses as low as possible during the ownership period, you should avoid mortgages with points.

Summary

1. Use a mortgage broker to help expose you to the maximum number of mortgage structures, rates, and terms and to give you advice on each. The financing vehicle you choose can have a significant impact on your financial success.

2. Minimize your down payment as long as your purchase price allows you to have "instant equity."

3. Mortgage debt is among the cheapest debt you can find.

4. A 30-year mortgage is the most stable and conservative way to finance your investment properties.

5. An adjustable rate mortgage (ARM), including "interest only" ARMs, can provide great cash flow benefits, but plan conservatively assuming a longer holding period.

6. Do not pay points on your mortgage.

Chapter 8 – The Tenant
Develop a business relationship, not a friendship

Ideal Scenario Alert: Rent to tenants with strong credit ratings and payment histories in order to maintain stable cash flow.

There are many tasks to execute once you have a signed contract and mortgage for your new property, but the most important is finding and accepting a quality tenant. Obviously, your monthly income is based on your tenant paying their rent and paying on time. This makes finding quality tenants who are able and committed to meeting their obligations to you a critical element in your success. Stated in the negative, having a tenant who DOES NOT pay on time, or at all, can create a nightmare scenario for a landlord. So, choose your tenants very carefully!

The good news is that you CAN distinguish between a reliable and unreliable tenant prior to entering into a lease agreement with them. It requires some focused up-front work on your part, but it is well worth the time and will take you a long way towards a fruitful, mutually beneficial, and fair relationship with your tenants, along with generating consistent and reliable cash flow.

Finding a Tenant

I have rented properties through licensed real estate agencies as well as through my own advertising and have found success with both. Perhaps in your first investment or two you will want to use a realtor, but once you build experience you may want to do your own marketing, or use both. Many residential real estate investors give realtors short shrift and choose not to involve them, often missing opportunities to find quality tenants as a result.

Some brokers take their fees from the tenants (making it zero cost to you to use them), others from property owners. I will say this much: If a real estate agent brings you a high quality, qualified, long-term tenant, their fee becomes a rounding error in the whole financial equation and is an excellent investment. Realtors can do professional background and credit checks on potential tenants, and while you want to do your own checking, having a potential resident who clears a realtor's hurdle is a great start. It also increases your odds of success of generating consistent cash flow.

My go-to advertising vehicle in the last ten years has been Craigslist. Listing your property on this free internet site can be all you need to find the quality tenant you are seeking. Most people looking to rent search its ads regularly. When advertising your rental property on Craigslist, be sure to do the following:

- Put the number of bedrooms and bathrooms in the title of the ad. Tenants usually search by community and bedroom quantity, and as such it is best to ensure that the title of your ad has the number of bedrooms and bathrooms (e.g. 2BR, or 2 Bedrooms). While this seems like basic blocking and tackling, you would be surprised at how uninformative some titles are.
- List surrounding towns in the body of your ad. While Craigslist automatically asks for the city or town of your property, it is a little-known trick to also list two or three surrounding towns at the bottom of your ad in order to draw potential tenants who are searching nearby communities. This widens the pool of people who can find your property and may just land you a tenant!
- Update your ad every week or two which ensures that it does not expire and keeps it at the top of search lists. Because Craigslist has so many ads, remaining near the top of the search results exposes you to many more potential tenants.

Keeping in mind the "pre-rent" concept you can list your property on Craigslist even before you officially own that property. It is best to inform the selling realtor that you are pre-listing the property in hopes of generating rental income immediately after closing. The selling realtor will, hopefully. allow you to take photos in advance of the closing on the property. You could also use the photos from the seller's listing as they are usually professionally done and represent the best image of the property itself. If you find a potential tenant and need to show them the property, the selling realtor will usually arrange escorted access for you and your potential tenants to visit the property.

Ideal Scenario Alert: The perfect execution of the purchase/rent timing is to have the tenant move in the day after closing. To pull off a real estate closing and tenant move-in on the same day is a cash flow home run!

The Four Categories of Tenants

In my many years of renting residential real estate, I have had generally four categories of tenants:

1. The first, best, and "ideal scenario" tenants are the ones who pay their rents religiously on the first of the month.
2. The second type are the laggards who mail in their rents on the first or second day of the month (arriving to you around the fifth of the month), which is acceptable.
3. The third are those irresponsible tenants who regularly pay their rents some time during the month, but typically not in the first five to seven days of the month. The date you receive the rent is random and almost always late, creating cash flow insecurity for you as the owner and mortgage holder.
4. The fourth is the disaster scenario: The tenants who do not pay for months at a time.

The "ideal" and the "laggard" tenants are acceptable and should be retained for as long as possible. The "irresponsible" tenants are manageable, especially if you are diligent about collecting your late fees assuming of course that you can cover your mortgage payment until you receive the rent check. The "disaster" tenants are to be avoided by all means possible.

Whatever category your tenant falls into, your mortgage provider will not be forgiving and will still expect your payment at the beginning of every month. Given this, it is critically important that you screen your tenants very, very carefully and that you do not accept any tenants without positive credit ratings and rental payment histories.

Screen your tenants very carefully! This sounds easy enough but it is an area that has tripped up many less-experienced real estate investors and, even at times, experienced ones like me. Some owners are so anxious to rent their properties that they short circuit the credit and reference process, often with awful results, at which time they look back with great regret. I cannot emphasize enough how critical it is to execute your due diligence during this critical stage.

Don't be tempted to rent quickly and circumvent the background process! These simple steps will help you find the right tenant:

- Ask your tenant for their credit rating documentation. Typically, credit card companies provide access to credit ratings, but also one free credit report from each of the credit reporting agencies is available to consumers annually. Tenants can request a copy of their credit report from Transunion, Experian, or Equifax.
- As an alternative, you can do a credit check on your potential tenant if they agree to let you do so. If you can avoid a problem tenant the $20 to $30 cost of the credit check could be the best money you ever spend. Some landlords charge an "application fee" to recover the cost of the credit check but I choose not to in order to make leasing my properties as painless as possible for my potential tenants.
- Request the names and phone numbers of the tenant's last two landlords. Be aware of a trick that has been pulled on me and probably other landlords, and that is the prospective tenant who provides you with the name and phone number of a friend or relative instead of the name of their landlord. When you call, they pretend to be the former landlord and provide a glowing review. Thus, be sure that the person you call is actually a former landlord!

Landlords generally want to help other landlords during this reference-checking process since they know how critical it is to rent to quality tenants in order to be successful in real estate investing. As you become an experienced investor you will find you want to help other landlords as well. When contacting the tenant's previous landlords ask the following questions:

1. How long did the tenant rent from you?
2. How much was the rent you charged? This question is important in that a tenant may have been great at paying a $1,200 monthly rent but, if your rent is $2,000, their payment history is less relevant.
3. What was their payment history? Were they ever delinquent? Why?
4. In what condition did they typically keep the home, both inside and out?
5. In what condition did they leave the home when they moved out?
6. Were there any complaints from neighbors during the time they rented from you?

7. Would you rent to them again?
8. Is there anything else you can share regarding these tenants?

Keep in mind that a late paying or delinquent tenant can turn into a terrible financial situation for you. Eviction laws greatly favor tenants so you could be stuck with a non-paying tenant for six to nine months. That's nine months during which you must pay your mortgage, insurance, and taxes with zero off-setting income. Avoid this at all costs by doing your homework up front!

You and your New Busines Partner, AKA Your Tenant

Once you find the right tenant, keep in mind that this is the start of a **business** relationship, not a **friendship.** As caring human beings, we are tempted to make friends with the people around us, including tenants living in our investment properties. But over the years I have learned that striking a balance between the "business" relationship and the "personal" relationship is very important in a rental situation. If you become very friendly with a tenant and they stop paying rent or are consistently late, it becomes a much more challenging situation to handle for both you and them from an emotional perspective. You feel badly because you are pressuring a "friend" and they feel somewhat betrayed that you are doing so and may take advantage of you. I have made this mistake in the past and it caused me to continue to give a tenant leeway over time and it eventually exploded into a major battle and eviction (story later in this chapter). I absorbed 15 months of zero rent before I unwound the situation I had gotten myself into. Following my informed advice will spare you from a similar experience, saving you thousands of dollars.

Collecting Rent

Ideal Scenario Alert: You receive your rental payments from your tenant on the first day of the month, every month, during their tenancy.

There are strategies that can help you manage cash flow and on-time rental receipt effectively. The natural tendency of quality tenants is to mail the rent on the first of the month, arriving in your mailbox anywhere from two to five days later. Add in the typical five to seven business days for a check to clear and before you know it you are pushing 12 to 15 days into the month. In Chapter 9, I describe various ways to structure the lease to collect tenants' rents sooner, but there are a few other steps you can take that do not involve the lease:

- Pick up the Rent. You can pick up the rent from the tenant on the first of the month (assuming the property is in reasonable proximity to your home). With one of my tenants, I call them at the end of the month and tell them I will pick up the check at a convenient time for them on the due date. While this may seem obtrusive and, in many cases may not be necessary, the fact of the matter is the rent is due on the first day of the month and all you are doing is asking to claim it on that very day.
- Invoice the Tenant. Another option is invoicing your tenant. I have tried this in the past and found it to be successful with some tenants. Some people like receiving invoices as it formalizes the business arrangement, and makes them more likely to pay on time. In these cases, I mailed the invoice on the 20th of the month for the next month's rent. The invoice can be a simple document but should include their name, your name, your mailing address, the amount of rent due, and the due date (the first of the month). At the bottom of the invoice, you should note in bold that "All rent received after the due date will incur a fee of $X as per our rental agreement."
- Offer Electronic Payment. You can also offer to accept rent payments electronically through Paypal, Venmo, or Zelle. Typically, payments made this way result in the money being immediately available to you in your checking account. It is a good practice to encourage payments to flow this way but be sure that you do not incur a transaction fee. For example, Paypal has two ways tenants can make payments: one is free and the other results in the receiver (you, the landlord) being charged a fee.

Lastly, it is critically important that the first time the tenant is late with their rent payment you claim the late fee. This is not so much about getting the extra money as it is a demonstration to the tenant that you are serious about enforcing the terms of the lease. You are establishing good habits in your relationship with your tenant and when they know right from the start that you will be unforgiving about late payments they will be less likely to pay late in the future.

This is really no different than how I raise my children. When I let them do something they should not, they feel free to do it again. When I punish them the first time they break a rule, they tend not to break it again. While your tenants obviously are not children, the same human condition applies; they will quickly learn that you will not tolerate delinquent payments without collecting the penalty fee. This doesn't have to be a battle; you simply invoice your tenants for the penalty fee and if they don't pay it, invoice them again, and if they don't pay after that call them and request the late payment fee. Note that the lack of payment of the fee is a violation of the lease agreement and you should feel comfortable and confident noting this to your tenant.

For the most part I have had outstanding tenants, but I have also had a few very bad experiences, including one terrible one that I am sharing in hopes that you will learn from my major miscues and save yourself from the consequences that I suffered.

****

My Personal Example: The Tenant Nightmare.
About 12 years ago, a man called me about a rental property I had on the market in a downtown location. The rent was $1,600 per month in a property zoned for commercial and residential use. I met him and his twenty-year-old son and liked them very much. They had plans to open a walk-up salad and soup restaurant on part of the first floor and live on the second floor. The business idea sounded good to me on the surface and, as I said, I liked them personally. He was also a pastor, so how bad could this be?
I was soon going to learn!

I executed a background check with one previous landlord that came back positive (in retrospect, I am not sure it was his former landlord, more likely a friend, a trick you should look out for). I did not do any other due diligence. I was anxious to rent the property because it had been vacant for two months.

After three months of consistent on-time rent payments, the tenant began renovations on the first floor for the take-out restaurant, including the addition of a commercial kitchen and walk-up window. The plans were impressive and he was enthusiastic, and I was rooting for him to succeed. I became personally and emotionally involved and even offered him advice, including reviewing his business plan.

Then it happened. With 75% of the renovations complete, he missed a

44

rent payment. I called him and he told me that it would come on the 15th of the month and he offered his apologies. The 15th came and went without a check. At this point, I arranged a meeting with him and he explained that he had received a larger than expected bill for some equipment and he was financially constrained. He needed 30 to 45 days to recover and, at that time, he would pay me all rent due. Liking and trusting him, and thinking too optimistically, I agreed to grant him more time.

The 45 days passed and all he sent me was a check for $500 and a note, "I'm trying my best." Now, $3,200 past due, my concern was increasing. I met with him again and he explained earnestly that he had income pending from multiple sources and that he would make good on his past and future rental payments. Given the way I had handled the relationship with him up to this point, it was like a friend pleading with a friend to give him more time. It was a situation and relationship structure of my own creation and it was difficult to escape.

Again, I agreed, but more skeptically. Two months later, now $6,400 delinquent plus penalty fees, I called him and he didn't answer. Over and over again I called and still no answer. He was avoiding me! Time to go see him in person.

After multiple trips to the property, I finally found him and we spoke face to face. He gave me $500 in cash and told me that a check for the full amount due was still pending. However, this time I told him I was going to take action to have him and his son evicted. While I was speaking with him, and as I looked around the first floor, it struck me that he had done three-quarters of a major renovation that would not be useful for any other tenant in the future. I would have to undo all the work to convert the property back to its original layout! The scope of the nightmare became clear to me.

I began the eviction process immediately. Nine months later, he was out. Nine months on top of five months, 14 months in total, with zero rent. And the tenant lived in the property the entire time. Keep in mind that during those 14 months, my mortgage provider had required, and received, my mortgage payment of $1,400 per month. That's $19,600 out of pocket during a time when the tenant only paid me $1,000. Even worse, I had to spend another $10,000 to undo the renovations.

This, my dear readers, was a completely avoidable nightmare. I mismanaged this relationship in nearly every important way. To add insult to injury, during my efforts to have him evicted, I learned of a past history that I could have easily found had I done even the slighted amount of due diligence on him. His background included a prison record!

****

What bit me here that I don't want to bite you?

1. I was too anxious to rent a property that had been vacant for two months. In retrospect, I would have been much better off waiting another month or two for the right tenant.
2. I did an insufficient background check.
3. I liked the prospective tenant personally (after 30 minutes of conversation) and this influenced my decision-making.
4. His profession led me to believe he would be a good tenant.
5. When he was delinquent in his payments early on, I was much too lenient, colored by the fact that I liked him and had become too close to him personally.
6. I should have started the eviction process sooner.

These mistakes cost me approximately $30,000. I have not made any such mistakes since, and now that you have read the story, you won't either. Fortunately, there is one happy fact in the whole scenario. After holding that property for ten years, I sold it for more than twice what I paid for it, and other than my one nightmare experience, I only had three months of total vacancy in the property during the entire ten-year period.

The nightmare story aside, I believe it is very important to treat your tenants well. View them as valuable, high-paying clients that you want to satisfy and retain. You should do this because it is obviously the right thing to do, but it is also a very good business practice in the long run. If you are responsive and attentive to your tenants, they will be more likely to pay their rents on time, take care of your property, and stay in your property for longer periods. Respond to their calls, fix the legitimate issues they raise, thank them when they pay their rents on time, send them holiday cards and small gifts, and make them feel respected and cared for.

Summary

1. Find your tenants through Craigslist or a reputable real estate firm.

2. Pre-rent (prior to closing) whenever possible to optimize cash flow.
3. Screen your tenants very carefully with no shortcuts.
4. Ensure your tenant knows you expect to receive rent payments on the first of the month and that you will not forgive late fees.
5. Your tenant/landlord relationship is a business relationship. Treat your tenants with respect and deal with them fairly but remember they are clients, not friends.
6. Don't hesitate to initiate the eviction process promptly if necessary.

Chapter 9 – The Lease
Lighten your load by giving your tenant more responsibilities

Residential real estate lease contracts are straightforward and easy to find on the internet or in "big box" office stores such as Staples. But it is the modifications you make to that lease that can change the nature of your landlord experience in a very positive way.

Your first step is to find a standard lease that meets the laws of your state. This is important as each state has different residential lease laws and you need a lease that conforms to your state's laws. I have purchased standard leases for my home state of New York from legalzoom.com as well as lawdepot.com (I have no affiliation with either company). The price for a base lease is usually less than $40 and you can customize these leases to add your own names, dates, rental amounts, and terms and conditions. The key areas to focus on are:

- Rental payment due date, incentives for on-time payment, and late fees.
- Lease start and end dates and the ability to renew.
- Renewal rental rate (increase).
- Maintenance issues, how they will be managed, and who will manage them.

Let's take these one at a time.

Rent Payment Due Date

The typical lease should require payment in full by the 1st of the month, without implying that because a late fee is not incurred until the 7th day that the tenant can wait seven days to make their payment. The disparity between your mortgage due date and the rental payment "end date" of seven days creates what I call "cash flow stress." Let's talk about how to relieve that stress!

One method I have used successfully over time is to tell the tenant that the 1st of the month is the rental due date and you expect the rent on that day. Do this politely but indicate to them early on that you expect rent on the first. You will be surprised that simply by behaving this way you will see the tenant adopting your philosophy and you will be much more likely to receive your payment on the 1st or close to it.

Tenants will read a landlord's attitude towards the due date early in the lease term and their behaviors will be shaped for the remainder of their tenancy, so do not show weakness here!

As we all know, many types of payments are due on the first of the month, such as car payments. Teach your tenant early on that yours has priority, that while they may not get a call on the first of the month from the bank financing their car, they will get a call from you. People naturally choose the path of least resistance and will pay their lease ahead of other obligations if you manage them effectively. You should be vigilant on this and call your tenant every month if you don't receive the payment by the 1st (you may choose to make it the 2nd, but not beyond that).

Another method I have used with great success is providing an incentive in the lease for on-time payment. Note that the incentive should be an amount that you are comfortable sacrificing relative to the lease payment. It doesn't take much, but a 1.5% to 2% discount surprisingly goes a long way. Sacrificing $50 on a $2,300 lease is no problem for me and a meaningful savings to my tenant. If my lease payment were $1,000, the $50 would be too large a portion of rent for me to forgo, in which case I could lower the incentive to something like $25. A tenant who pays $1,000 is likely to value $25 as much or more as the tenant who pays $2,300 values $50. These incentives have proven very effective for me and I'm confident they will work for you!

****

A Personal Example

For one lease, I offered a $50 rent reduction on the monthly rent if I received payment on the 1st of the month. My tenant took advantage of this almost every month with his check often arriving at the end of the previous month, so he was sure to get the discount! The rent was $2,300 per month and I was happy to sacrifice $50 to know that my tenant had prioritized payment to me above all others, relieving my "cash flow stress." This method requires strict enforcement though. In one instance, his check arrived on the 2nd of the month with the $50 discount. In order to set the proper precedent, I told him that, unfortunately, his check had arrived on the 2nd and, therefore, he owed an additional $50 in rent. He was not ever late after that! If I had given him leeway at that time, he was likely to take advantage of it in the future as well and the arrival dates of future payments would slip.

****

Length of Lease

Determining the length of the lease obviously requires the agreement of both parties, but as the landlord you should consider it very carefully. My experience is that with some tenants I wish I had a five-year lease, and with others I wish I had never signed a lease at all.

While some of you will have varying objectives for your properties (e.g. some may want to flip the property in a year, others to keep the property for ten years or more), my recommendation is to plan a retention period of five years or more. In such a case, I would sign a one-year lease with an option after the first six months (or 12 months) to extend the lease for up to three years. This way you can develop a reading on the quality of your tenant and their payment habits before you lock yourself into a three-year relationship with them. Do you have a great paying tenant who cares for your home? Sign them to a long-term lease. Have a tenant who is late and seems not to care for your property? Give yourself the option to move on after the one-year anniversary.

In addition to carefully considering the term of the tenancy, I put a placeholder in the lease that allows for a reasonable annual increase in the rent at my sole discretion. This recognizes my increasing costs (usually taxes and insurance increase from one year to the next). Based on my experience, costs increase approximately 2% to 4% so build such increases into your lease. 3% is fair and typical. Thus, you will add a term to the lease that says, "Lease will be subject to a 3% increase at each annual anniversary."

Just to reiterate my earlier assertion, a quality tenant is absolute gold, a poor tenant can be a nightmare. Don't let the latter situation be allowed to linger in your property any longer than legally necessary! By the same token, nurture and give special care to your quality tenants to encourage them to continue their lease arrangements with you.

Month to Month Leases

Ideal Scenario Alert: Do not have more than two to three months of vacancy during your ownership period.

There will be times when you and/or your tenant want to have the flexibility to exit the lease with 30 days' notice. For instance, if you have a 12-month lease with a tenant, the typical lease will say "in lieu

50

of a mutually agreed-to lease extension at the end of the 12-month term, the lease converts to a month-to-month lease. As such, either party can terminate the lease with 30 days' notice."

> *Examples: I have had two properties in two different month-to-month lease situations.*
>> o *The first property was one I was trying to sell. I was confident it was the type of property where the new buyer would want to live in the house herself, or lease to her own tenant. Therefore, I left the lease on a month-to-month in order to give the potential buyer the flexibility to do what they wanted with it. The new buyer could terminate the lease with 30 days' notice, or they could try to sign the current tenant for an additional 12 months. The important thing was the buyer had the option for either.*
>> o *The second was a property where I was looking for another tenant because the current one had been an inconsistent payer of her monthly rent. The month-to-month allowed me to collect rent while still looking for a tenant that was more likely to pay consistently.*

The "Low Touch" Landlord

Ideal Scenario Alert: Assign as much property management responsibility as possible to your tenant.

One of the most common fears of someone contemplating investing in residential real estate is the work and stress that is involved in caring for the tenant and the property. "I don't want to be a landlord," people will say. Most certainly being a landlord generates extra work and you should be prepared to do that work or to pay someone 15% to 20% of your rental income to manage the property for you. As busy as I am with my "day job," I don't pay a property manager because I don't want to lose that 20%. So, what can busy people like you and me do to properly care for our tenants and property while keeping the time commitment to a minimum? It turns out there are a few tools that I have written into leases that minimize the time I spend on my properties.

The first is what I have termed the "tenant calls" provision. Under this concept, the tenant is responsible for arranging the times and dates for a plumber, electrician, or carpenter to come to the property and fix what is broken. This is good for you because you don't need to get involved unless the issue is major; it is good for your tenant because they can go directly to the skilled professional, describe the problem, and arrange a convenient time for them to have the person come fix the issue. Most tenants embrace this approach because it gets them faster service at more convenient times, with accurate understandings of the problem at hand. You do need to have a set of skilled tradesmen whom you trust to be responsive to your tenants and to charge you fairly for the work they do. The side benefit is that the tradesmen who get a lot of business from you will be a lot more responsive to your tenants' calls and will do the job faster so the whole process works better. You win, your tenant wins, and the tradesmen win.

An example of the terms I put into my leases is:

"In the event of a plumbing, electrical, or structural issue, Tenant will email or call the Landlord to notify Landlord of the issue. Tenant will then be responsible to call the designated professional to arrange a mutually convenient time for service, and the tenant will be present while such services are executed by the technician. These designated professionals are: John Smith, plumber, phone 222.222.2222; Mary Johnson, electrician, phone 333.333.3333; Kim Carter, carpenter, phone 444.444.4444.

Making this language part of your lease will save you much time and effort.

The second method for reducing your time commitment, and potential expenses, is to purchase appliances with five-year extended warranties. While many consumer advocates say that extended warranties on dishwashers, refrigerators, washing machines, dryers, and ranges are not cost effective, in the case of real estate investment I highly recommend them and use them as a rule.

The benefit to extended warranties is evident in the following example.

> *I purchased new appliances at Lowe's for two properties, and with each I purchased the five-year extended warranty for an additional $100 per appliance. This tax-deductible expense (making the real cost more like $60*

per appliance) defined for me the expenses for each of these appliances for the next five years. I had no worries about an unexpected major repair expense, giving me confidence in my consistent cash flow. As I'm sure you know, appliance service calls can be very expensive and inconvenient, and none of us likes an unexpected $250 to $500 expense for an appliance repair. I simply factor the extended warranty costs into my financial analysis and never think of that expense again.

It is important to ensure your lease contains references to this warranty arrangement such as the language I include.

"In the event the washing machine, dryer, refrigerator, dishwasher, or range is not functioning properly, Tenant will call Lowe's Warranty Service at 666.666.6666 and arrange a mutually convenient time for repair. Tenant will then be present when the Lowe's technician is present on the property."

The inclusion of the "tenant calls" provision and the extended warranties solves two traditional landlord issues. One is the fear of an unexpected expense, and the other is the need to get involved in appliance repair issues. The tenant calls Lowe's, the tenant meets Lowe's for the repair, and you are not impacted in any way.

It is important to note that my tenants actually like having these provisions in their leases. While they may have questions when they initially see the terms in the lease, once I take the time to explain to them the benefits of this approach, they generally accept these terms. I have also found that once the tenants have an incident or two, and I ask them their opinion about this "tenant calls" process versus "landlord calls," they express great satisfaction with the "tenant calls." They report that they can arrange a schedule that is more convenient for themselves, avoid having the landlord enter their home (often without them being present), and generally get the repair done in a timelier manner than they otherwise would. This is truly a win-win, you will be glad you put these provisions in your leases!

Summary
1. Use a lease for your state of residence but modify it to ease your workload and cash flow pressure.
2. Make it clear to your tenant that rent is due on the 1st of the month; potentially add an incentive for an on-time payment.

3. Lock up quality tenants for longer lease terms, questionable tenants for shorter terms.
4. Add a provision for a 2% to 4% annual increase in rental rates in a multi-year lease.
5. Become a "Low-Touch" landlord.

Chapter 10 – About Renovations
Upgrade a property for higher rental prices and higher resale value

There are many instances when investing in a property that needs renovations can generate significant profits. I'm not talking about "flipping" houses as I am not a believer in such transactions as most "flips" are at the very low-end of the market where profits are thin. Renovating a property, however, can mean the ability to demand higher rental rates, as well as a higher selling price when it comes to cashing out of your investment.

I'm going to cover three categories of renovations:

1. Purchasing a property and performing a major renovation
2. Purchasing a property and performing relatively minor upgrades
3. An in-between the two where only moderate renovation is required.

Major Renovations or Complete Overhaul
There are unique investment opportunities to purchase a property at a well below market price, but then must spend a significant amount of capital in order to transform the property into a modern, attractive, high quality home that will draw significant rental income. Complete overalls typically require redoing the kitchen, bathrooms, much of the plumbing, and the wiring.

When purchasing a property that needs major renovations it is critical to calculate an appropriate purchase price. Consider:

- Estimated market value of the property in a fully renovated condition, *minus*
- Purchase price, *minus*
- Renovation cost, *minus*
- 15% of the renovation cost as the contingency for under-estimating the cost of renovations, *equals*
- Total "instant equity" of the property

These are investment situations rife with risk and opportunity! The fact that a home needs major renovation gives you as the buyer leverage to drive down your purchase price, often creating an opening for you to complete the renovations and have instant equity. However, if you pay too high a price for the home and you under-estimate the cost of the renovations, you could have "instant *negative* equity," which is, of course, highly undesirable. Thus, it is crucial to estimate renovation costs carefully, seek input and quotes from skilled construction professionals, and build in 15% contingency for unforeseen costs that may arise.

****

A Personal Example
Major Renovations, The Gut and Overhaul

In 2015, my wife and I acquired the side-by-side two-family pictured on the cover of this book. Both units were in terrible shape and needed full renovations, including all new wiring and circuit breakers, plumbing and heating systems, complete overhauls of the bathrooms and kitchen, and more. We gutted the house and renovated it top to bottom. It took six months to complete, but at the end we were able to rent both sides to outstanding tenants at very favorable rates. When we put the house on the market we were overwhelmed by the interest from potential buyers. Here are the numbers from this renovation:

Purchase Price	**$440,000**
Renovation Cost	**$295,000**
Total Cost	**$735,000**
Rental Income per month	
(all utilities paid by tenants)	**$5,900**
Annual Rental Income	**$70,800**

In aggregate across both units in the last five years, we have had only one month of vacancy. The house would also likely sell today for somewhere between $810,000 and $900,000.

****

Minor Renovations and Upgrades

I have found that relatively inexpensive upgrades can mean that a property rents more quickly, and for a higher rate, than without the upgrades. For example, replacing a refrigerator, dishwasher, microwave, and range will make a huge difference aesthetically in a kitchen, yet only cost $2,500 or less. Even stainless-steel appliances which are typically very appealing to potential tenants are available at great prices.

Other upgrades, such as re-tiling a bathroom, replacing a sink, toilet, bathtub, or washer/dryer, can make a huge difference to potential tenants.

The least expensive upgrade with the highest impact per dollar spent is paint. Unless the interior has been painted in the previous two years and had very light use over that time, painting is almost always a good idea. This is especially true for great rooms, dining rooms, master bedrooms, and family rooms that have lots of wall space (versus walls with many windows) and visible wood trim.

Painting is also a task you can handle yourself if you are so inclined. Consider painting key rooms when the house is empty right after you buy it or between the expiration of one lease and the potential start of another.

The benefits of these minor upgrades are four-fold:

- First, the improvements could land you a tenant 30 to 60 days sooner than you might have otherwise. The photos in your advertisements not only show the upgrades but you should also tout them in the description of your property. If you are renting a property for $2,000 a month, renting 60 days sooner means $4,000 in rent that you would not have obtained otherwise, more than paying for the upgrades.
- Second, you may be able to command more rent because of the upgrades and/or renovations. For example, if you can obtain $100 to $200 more in rent, you would bring in $1,200 to $2,400 more in rent per year. Tenants compare properties and seeing one with new kitchen appliances versus one without, would almost certainly put your property at an advantage.
- Third, because you have new appliances (or other new items), you will incur less in maintenance expenses -- new breaks less often than old, and new usually includes a warranty or guarantee of some kind.

- Fourth, when you are ready to sell your property you can command a higher price or you might sell sooner than you would have without the upgrades. A higher price makes the changes well worth the investment.

****

A Personal Example
Minor Renovations

I purchased a single-family home in a nice quiet neighborhood in an adjacent town to where I live. The house was in good condition and had been well-maintained by a young couple who had owned it for five years. But the kitchen appliances appeared to be 15 years old and were white. White appliances don't wear well over time and these looked discolored. The family room had what can only be defined as "dirty" walls with fingerprints, nail holes, and chipped wood trim. This house was ready to rent in the condition I bought it, but it was clear that with an investment of $1,750 in black appliances and some paint for the family room would mean higher likelihood of renting the property. I executed these tasks, all within one week, and the house was rented two weeks later. In this case, I am convinced that I rented the house weeks earlier than I would have otherwise, and that I was able to command $200 or more in monthly rent based on the upgrades. This made the upgrades well worthwhile!
****

Moderate Renovations and Upgrades

Moderate renovation projects can include whole new kitchens and fully renovated bathrooms. These projects require thoughtful financial analyses to determine their payback period and whether they are worth doing. Included in such an analysis would be:
1. The cost of the renovations measured against additional rent you might command, or the additional resale value when it comes time to sell the property.
2. Rental downtime or lag to sell time. Renovating a bathroom or a kitchen may take weeks or even months, during which time you cannot collect rent nor are you likely to have your property on the market. Time in this case is money!

3. The "intangible" benefits of the upgrades, including the increased attractiveness of the property that might drive more interest from potential tenants or buyers, allowing me to rent the property sooner and for higher rent. I have seen many articles in home improvement magazines about the financial benefits of certain upgrades, but many fail to take into account these intangibles which, in the end, translate into more income, or income generated sooner than it might have been otherwise.

In my experience I have found that fully renovated kitchens have the highest impact on your property's value. This may seem obvious to you, but many of my competitors do not understand this. Kitchens often are the key to winning a rental or a sale versus losing one. If I acquire a property with a kitchen that hasn't been renovated in the last four to five years, I will almost always renovate to some degree (maybe just installing new appliances), and often I will do a full end-to-end renovation.

****

A Personal Example
Moderate Renovations

I acquired a condominium that was in very good condition except for the master bathroom, which had very old white 4"x4" tile throughout, an old white tub that was discolored, had permanent rust stains around the drain and faucets that appeared to have been made in the late 1800s. The remainder of the house had been updated within the last five years. To upgrade the master bathroom, I invested $7,000 for tile, a new tub, faucets, sink, and cabinet, and $4,000 in labor. When I put the condominium on the market three or four potential tenants, including the one who rented it, commented specifically on how beautiful and new the master bathroom was! I leased the property in a mere two days.
****

Renovations and Interior Design
I have learned over time that when renovating an investment property it is important to think more "neutral" than "fancy." It is best to decorate with more traditional colors and designs versus taking chances with unique colors and designs. A more generic design direction may not thrill potential tenants but they are more likely to rent than the "turned off" client who has a very different taste from yours. This doesn't mean you have to be completely plain, but your best bets

for the broadest appeal is to paint walls and trim in light, off-white colors, paint or install lighter kitchen cabinets, and go white or grey on exteriors with black or dark grey roof tiles. Keep in mind your prospective tenants have their own furniture, paintings, photographs. Neutral colors will ensure that there won't be a clash. I have actually had potential tenants say "all of our furniture will go with this color perfectly!" when the walls were bone white.

If you do have a property that is in a unique location, such as the beach or the mountains, it is a good idea to incorporate some regional styles into your design. However, unless you are getting premium rent, be careful not to over-spend and end up with an asset whose cost is out of line with the income you can generate, and with an interior design that is difficult for the tenant to work with.

In conclusion, think carefully about renovations before you purchase a property. Some properties will simply need to be cleaned, most will need at least minor renovations, and some may need a major overhaul. The cost of these renovations is important to consider as you calculate the purchase price, as well as the impact the renovations may have your finding quality tenants who will pay a price that produces positive cash flow and profits throughout your ownership period.

Summary
1. Carefully consider renovation plans before purchasing a property and add the costs into the acquisition cost when doing your calculations of the value of such a property.
2. Renovations can be major, minor, or moderate (in between the major and minor). Each have different characteristics and understanding each is important as you build your real estate portfolio. Major overhauls present significant opportunities, but also prevent risks, so do your calculations carefully prior to purchasing
3. Be sure to build a 15% contingency cost in your renovation estimates to account for potential over-runs.
4. Bathrooms and kitchens tend to be the most renovated areas of investment properties. They also tend to have the highest impact on your ability to rent as well as the resale value and at what rate.
5. New kitchen appliances, especially in stainless steel, provide a desirable look that can land quality tenants sooner and potentially for higher rent.

6. Neutral colors are the best choice in order to attract the largest number of tenants.

Chapter 11 – Airbnb and VRBO
Rent on a short-term basis using online applications

In the past ten years, the short-term rental by online application – Airbnb and VRBO for example – has exploded. Many people have successfully rented their properties this way, and I've been one of them. I own a very high-end property that I rent using these online applications, generating more than $150,000 per year in rental income.

Investing in properties that rent for one to four weeks is a unique endeavor, very different from investing in long-term rental properties. Vacation homes located in on beaches and lakes, in the mountains and popular tourist destinations can be ideal for short term rentals.

****

A Personal Example, Part 1
I am fortunate enough to own a beautiful lakefront property in the Adirondack Mountains in upstate New York. I originally purchased this property as a vacation home for my family, but after testing short-term rental waters, I learned that there was high demand for such properties and plenty of profit to be made. I began by using "Vacation Rental By Owner", or VRBO (commonly pronounced, "verb-oh"), at www.vrbo.com. I took the time to write a detailed but concise summary about my property, noting every amenity, and uploaded high-definition photos. Within six months, I found that demand was so high that I had to turn renters away in large numbers, especially during the summer months. I turned away two potential renters for every guest I rented to! In order to rent the house in the off season, I also listed the property on Airbnb, thereby broadening my audience and attracting even more guests.

****

Evaluating a Short-Term Rental Investment
If you have found a property that is in a vacation hot-spot and likely to attract short-term guests, you need to do a serious evaluation of that property prior to purchase. For example:
1. In what season are you most likely to rent the property? If you are looking at a property in the area of Aspen, Colorado, you want to consider that you are likely to get most of your guests, and highest rates, during the winter and early spring. As

such you should estimate your weekly rental rate assuming you will have the highest occupancy from mid-December through March. You should also assume that the demand will be low or non-existent during the months of April through June, higher during July and August (but not as high as winter), and then light again the further you get into the fall. Given the seasonal nature of demand and its impact on occupancy and rates, be sure to account for this fluctuation and build in allowances for weeks when the home will go unrented. Prepare yourself for lumpy cash flow, high in some weeks and low or non-existent in other weeks, sometimes for very long stretches of time. Therefore, it is important to save some of the excess money you earn during the high demand weeks to ensure you can meet your expenses during the low demand weeks. This does not mean you can't generate a profit, but you have to plan your cash flows in and out to avoid stress during low demand (and therefore, low-income) periods.

2. Short-term rentals require significant coordination as you will have new guests "back to back" sometimes with only hours in between. Prepare for significant work (or invest in a caretaker/cleaner) for the days when your unit transitions from one guest checking out to another guest checking in.

****

A Personal Example, Part 2

I rent the Adirondack property during June, July, and August for seven days at a time, Saturday to Saturday, which is standard for most short-term vacation rentals in the area. I have guests leaving at 11 A.M., and new ones checking in at 4 P.M., every Saturday which means the house has to be fully checked, cleaned, and, repairs made if necessary, during a five-hour period. I do this every week from mid-June through the end of September.

****

Compare the rates and occupancies of the unit you are considering buying and of those nearby, especially those of similar quality, strategic location (e.g. on the water), and size. The more homework you do the more likely you are to make a successful and profitable investment.

3. Is the short-term rental property near your home so that you can address any issues that may arise during a guest's stay or after they check out and before the new guest checks in. If the

property is more than 45 minutes or an hour away, you should be certain you have a reliable caretaker to look after your property for you.

VRBO vs. Airbnb

There is much material available online describing VRBO and Airbnb and the advantages and disadvantages of each. It may be helpful, however, to have my perspective as a user of both. This is my opinion, based on my experience. If you choose to list a short-term rental property with either of these providers or any of the others listed online, I recommend you do your due-diligence on both.

My experience with VRBO is that it allows me to screen my potential guests more closely than Airbnb in advance of renting to them. It provides detailed reviews of potential guests from other landlords like me, describing how those guests behaved when they rented their properties. Airbnb feels more like a "take all comers" application, especially with its "Instant Booking" feature. Essentially if someone wants to rent your property, they can just book it without an opportunity for you to decide if they will be a fit for your property. While many people are fine with this, it certainly does not work for my high-value property. One irresponsible guest could easily do $10,000 or more in damage. I do not rent the house for a college fraternity getaway or a bachelor/bachelorette party. I much prefer large families, or to families having a reunion or celebrating a milestone.

I also find Airbnb more difficult to navigate and less robust, making it difficult to communicate the strengths and benefits of a particular property. Their property description section limits the amount of information you can provide on your property, and they limit the number of photos you can upload. To their credit, however, I will say that when we had a damage claim against a guest, Airbnb was very fair in their resolution, covering the approximate $6,000 in costs for the repair.

****
Personal Example, Part 3
While most of my guests discover the property and book via VRBO, I had a guest rent through Airbnb in early 2020. Because I find it more difficult to screen potential guests and their reasons for renting the property I ended up with a problematic guest. While the house sleeps up to 20, we believe he invited 24 to 26 people. Upon checkout, there

were five large construction bags full of beer bottles and beer cans. Worst of all, the French doors to the patio were destroyed, pushed out instead of in. I brought this issue to the guest and asked him what happened. He claimed not to know what I was referring to. I filed a claim with Airbnb for the damage, and thankfully they reimbursed us for the cost of the repairs.

****

Overall, I recommend both services, but be very thoughtful about whom you rent to, their purposes, and read carefully any "guest" reviews posted by other owners on the two online applications.

About Discrimination

While I am very thoughtful about whom I rent to, I want to be clear that I do not discriminate in any way. The only things I take into consideration are the reason for the rental, the number of people included in the rental party, and reviews posted by other owners about guests' prior behavior. VRBO and Airbnb correctly have very strict discrimination policies and I follow them to the letter -- you should, too.

Summary

1. The financial evaluation of short-term rental properties should take into consideration seasonality of rentals and the possibility for inconsistent cash flows.
2. The workload with short term properties can be significant due to the short amount of time between guests checking out and those checking in.
3. Choose a property close to home so that you can manage it, or hire a property manager/caretaker.
4. VRBO and Airbnb are the two most common methods for renting short term properties. In my experience, VRBO provides more flexibility with posting your listing and for screening renters.

Chapter 12 – Cashing Out
Claim your prize

Ideal Scenario Alert: Sell High! Selling price shows a 5% per year increase in the value of your property.

The time has come for you to harvest the juiciest fruits of your great work and sell your property. Why are you doing so? Perhaps you would like the cash for an addition to your home, to pay college tuition, or you would like to acquire a larger or smaller investment property in a different location. Whatever the reason, you want to proceed with the last phase of the ideal scenario by selling high and selling in a reasonable time frame. Hopefully, in addition to positive cash flow and profit during your rental phase, you have experienced significant appreciation in the value of your asset. That appreciation is composed not only of the "instant equity" you generated at the purchase but also significant market-based appreciation due to increasing home values. You've done great so far but you have one last and very important step to make your investment a home run from start to finish: Sell at the highest price!

When to Sell

Of course, you want to sell at a time of strength, both in relation to the real estate market and your personal financial situation. When the market is strong, prices are high, so if you can sell during a strong market and when you are not under pressure to sell immediately, you will generate maximum profits. These factors won't always align but, if you plan and are thoughtful, you can adjust the timing of your sale for maximum profitability. Be thinking well in advance of the date (months, or even a year) when you want to sell so that you are not under pressure to sell into a weak market or pressured to take a lower price than you might want or deserve for your property.

Sell your property at a time when the market is strong, and you don't have financial pressures. This allows you to make unemotional decisions on offers made on your property and to maximize the sale price. Don't find yourself needing to sell quickly!

You should also consider the end of the lease date of your current tenant when determining when to sell. As previously mentioned, if you think that your property is more likely to be purchased by someone who will be using it as their residence, you want the existing tenant's lease to be on a month-to-month renewal at the time of the sale (versus a lease that expires far into the future) so that your buyer can move in upon closing should they choose to do so.

If an investor is more likely to buy the property and rent it for similar rates as yours and you have a quality tenant and solid rental income, it can sometimes be better to have a longer lease term with the existing tenant. You can also sell this as an "advantage" to an investor, telling them that if they buy they will have a built-in tenant who pays their rent on time and who wants to stay for the long term.

My experience has been that the vast majority of buyers of my properties want to know that they have the option to retain the existing tenant or to terminate the lease in a short period of time. They seem to like the flexibility this provides to them. Their motivations vary but some think they can generate a higher rental income, others have pre-determined tenants, some want to move in themselves, or, in a two-family, they may want to move into one unit and rent the other.

Whatever the reasons, you will find that having tenants on month-to-month leases are more desirable to a larger set of buyers and, therefore, you want to factor the expiration of leases into your selling plan. If you are anticipating selling in the subsequent 12 to 18 months, plan your leases and their end dates accordingly.

Don't get stuck with a buyer who very much wants to purchase your property at a price you would be happy to accept, but who won't buy because you have timed your lease end dates poorly and have not given the buyer the flexibility they desire.

****
A Personal Example
In anticipation of the potential sale of a two-family property, I had tenants in both properties on a month-to-month basis. When I put the property on the market, sure enough I had a buyer who wanted to occupy one of the units and rent the other. I was able to terminate the lease on the unit he wanted to live in, and I helped the buyer sign up the existing tenant in the other unit for a one-year lease. The buyer was very excited to learn that he had the flexibility to do exactly what he wanted and not lose a day of rent from the unit he had planned to rent. In addition, he didn't have to do all the work to find a new tenant who

may not have been as consistent in their on-time payments as the existing tenant was. I'm convinced that in this case I wouldn't have sold the property otherwise, or I wouldn't have received as high a price. The situation worked out very well for me and the buyer!

****

Choosing a Realtor to Sell your Property

It may seem unnecessary to say this but choosing the right realtor for the sale matters even more significantly than choosing the realtor to help you buy. I state this somewhat obvious point because in Chapter 3 I write that it is not necessary to have a realtor to purchase a property. But in the case of selling your property the realtor is almost always a crucial factor in your success in selling at the highest possible price.

A foundational point is to use a reputable real estate firm with a brand name that is prevalent in your community and nearby communities. Find the strongest two or three brands and then find the realtor within one of those firms who is going to deliver the results you want. Different firms have different reputations and one town may be dominated by one real estate firm while the adjacent town is dominated by a different firm. Determine who the leader is in your area, find their most successful selling realtor, and sign them up!

As you seek out your realtor of choice, keep in mind that there are generally three types of realtors:

- Those who are successful because they **list** many properties.
- Those who are successful because they **sell** a lot of properties.
- Those who both **list** and **sell** many properties.

Realtors in the 2nd and 3rd categories are the ones you want. I say this because I know many realtors who are great at convincing people to list their properties with them. While this may be one indicator of their sales capabilities, it does not necessarily mean they are great at **selling** properties. I know several realtors who make a living piling up listings but who don't effectively market and close on properties they have listed; they let other realtors make the sales. Remember, listing realtors are paid at least half of the commission upon the sale of a house they have listed, even if they don't lift a finger after it's been put on the market! You want a listing realtor who "sells." Focus on this key point in your interviews as well as their performance relative to other real estate agents. How do they rank versus other realtors in their office, and other realtors in the area? This is simple blocking and tackling. Investing time in finding the right professional will pay off in a higher selling price, a faster sale, and increased profit. Once you identify a realtor who is successful for you on a transaction, you can use that same person on subsequent ones.

A very common mistake in choosing a realtor is selecting a friend, or a friend of a friend, as your listing/selling realtor. I warned of this error earlier when choosing a realtor to help you with a purchase, and the same applies when you are selling. DO NOT CHOOSE A REALTOR BECAUSE THEY ARE A RELATIVE OR A FRIEND OR A FRIEND OF A FRIEND! The first issue that can arise when you do choose a friend as your realtor is that you obviously want the best, not the nicest, selling your home. The second issue is, once you realize you have chosen an ineffective realtor and for the wrong reasons, it becomes very difficult to address the issue. You do not want to be cracking down on your realtor/neighbor, criticizing them, or even firing them. Similar to the "business relationship" we recommend for dealing with tenants, the seller/realtor relationship needs to be a business relationship as well. Choose a realtor who has a crystal-clear track record of successfully selling properties.

Real Estate Commissions

Having recommended that you use a realtor when selling your property, I want to share an important point about real estate commissions. In my earliest experiences, I wanted to pay the lowest commissions possible to the realtors involved in my transactions. My thinking was: The lower the commission, the higher my profit, right? Not necessarily! Realtors need to be incented to sell the property and to put in as much time, attention, and advertising as they can. I have seen commissions ranging from 3.5% to 6% but in my experience any realtor accepting 4% or less is likely not a quality realtor and I recommend that you avoid them. The most common commissions today are somewhere between 4.5-6%, the average is 5%.

****

A Personal Example

I was selling a $300,000 property and could pay a realtor 3.5% ($10,500) or as high as 6% ($18,000). On the surface, I had an $7,500 dilemma that was easily resolved by going with the lower commissioned realtor. But what service was I going to get for that 3.5% and how hard were my agent (and other agents) going to work to sell a property for a $10,500 commission versus an $18,000 commission?

Surely, they would work harder on the $18,000 opportunity, focusing more time, effort, and advertising investment on it. Not only that, realtors have lots of properties on the market they can sell and when choosing which ones to focus their limited time on, they will choose those that generate the highest income for them. I have on a few occasions even offered realtors a "bonus" above and beyond the 6% commission. A bonus is very effective, resulting in realtors focusing on selling my property as their top priority.

In this case, I believed the realtor would be sufficiently incented to sell my property if I negotiated the commission from 6% down to 5.5%.

She accepted the reduced rate and sold my property in a very short period of time to a quality buyer who closed promptly. I used that same realtor in future transactions at commissions of 5.5%. While the 5.5% was higher than industry average of 5%, the quality of service I received and the increased prices my properties commanded due to the effectiveness of the realtor made this .5% premium worth paying.

****

If you are selling a lower-priced property you may want or need to pay a higher commission. For instance, if you were selling a property for $90,000, realtors may demand a minimum 6% commission, because a 4 or 5% commission may not make it worth their time. A 5% commission on a $300,000 sale ($15,000) is a lot different than 5% commission on a $100,000 sale ($5,000). Therefore, expect realtors to request higher percentage commissions on lower priced sales. The counter to that is true as well: If you have a $2,000,000 property to sell, you should request a commission rate-- even 4% of that amount is an $80,000 commission!

Selling Without a Realtor

I have had a few experiences trying to sell a property without a realtor, although I have never actually closed a sale that way. In general, I have found that by-owner sales tend to attract a different and lower quality buyer and often produce prospective buyers who consume a lot of your time but never close. What you save in commissions, you will lose in the time and effort to find a buyer. Hire a great realtor, collaborate with them, and get your property sold at the right price. Close the deal efficiently and quickly High-performing selling realtors are worth the expense!

Establishing Your Listing Price

You have chosen your realtor, you have provided proper incentives, and now you need to establish your purchase price. My experiences have taught me that at this point it is crucial that you be very closely engaged with your realtor, challenging them and allowing them to challenge you, as you work through the highest possible sellable price. Otherwise, you could leave a lot of money on the table, costing you thousands or even tens of thousands of dollars.

I have friends who, in a buyer's market (slow sales environment) sold their houses very quickly. "I sold my house in one day!" they proudly exclaim. The first thought that goes through my mind is "I'm happy for you but you sold at too low a price and left money on the table." If you are selling your house in just one day in an average or slow market, you almost certainly set your price too low.

How do you establish your asking price? Homework. Do your homework, working closely with your chosen realtor. I have never listed a property for the first price that a realtor suggested. In conjunction with my realtor, I look at the comparable (comps) sales and listings and help her identify the comps that most effectively support a higher asking price. My realtors and I usually identify 10 to 12 comps, which I then narrow down to the 5 or 6 highest priced homes that most resemble my property. You can use a mix of comps, some that show an asking price and some that show sold prices. Your realtor can use these comps as evidence with potential buyers that your price is a fair one. You should keep in mind, however, that sold prices mean more than asking prices. It is one thing to ask for a certain price and another to sell at that price.

You can price a property too low and lose profit as a result. But you can also set the price too high. There is a fine line between an aggressively high price and a too-high price. Work with your realtor, get to the high end but within reason and with evidence to back it up, and then gauge the market's reaction. A property priced too high will likely sit for months and never sell at that price, forcing you to lower your price, which tends to taint the property as a "house that won't sell." This then leads to a further reduction in price, and so on. It is a cycle you must avoid. In addition, tenants don't like living in houses that are for sale. It creates uncertainty for them, wondering if the new buyer will want them to stay or to go, and they may vacate the property leaving you without rental income during the time when you have the house on the market. This vacancy could last months, leaving you with a mortgage payment, insurance, and taxes to pay without any offsetting income from a tenant.

To avoid these complications, establish three prices in collaboration with your realtor. All three are very important because they will become the benchmarks by which you will make decisions regarding the sale and the offers you receive.

- Your target price (What you want to sell for).
- Your asking price (What you will list it for).
- Your bottom-line price (The lowest price you will accept).

My general rules are that my target price be approximately 5% below the asking price and my bottom-line price be approximately 10% below my asking price. These are dependent on market conditions, the strength of my desire to sell, and the time frame in which I want to sell. The discipline required here is similar to that of when you initially buy a property. You must know where you are headed, what your goals and limits are, and you must stick with them.

****

A Personal Example

I listed a property for $395,000. My target price was $380,000 and my bottom-line price was $369,000. These three reference prices acted as a roadmap for me as I worked through the selling and offer review process. I sold the property for $379,000 after having it on the market for a month and a half.

****

Offers

All offers should be considered in line with your three reference prices. As the saying goes, "If you don't know where you are going, you will probably end up somewhere else." The reference prices you establish are "Where you are going." When you receive offers that are below these prices, try to bring the offer up with a counteroffer that still gives you room to close at a price in your desired range. Ideally, you own a quality property, have tenants on month-to-month leases, and are under no pressure to sell below your targets. It is a beautiful thing when time is on your side and a buyer wants to buy but you aren't desperate to sell. I call that "selling from strength."

****

A Personal Example

I set an asking price of $395,000 for a property, with my bottom-line price at $375,000. My target price was $380,000. The first offer came

72

in at $365,000. I thought, "OK, good enough to work with; let's see if I can get them in my range." I countered at $389,000 with an eye towards settling at $380,000. They countered with $370,000. Given this was early in the selling process, I was not going to get too aggressive, so I countered with $385,000. They stuck with their offer. I decided to stick with my $385,000. The seller disappeared, which happens all the time and is acceptable, but often they disappear and come back! And so it was in this case. Two weeks later, they came back and offered $381,000. Done! Note, had they not come back, I would not have chased them and, instead would have prepared for the next negotiation with a different buyer.

To Summarize:

Asking:	**$395,000**
Buyer Offer #1	**$365,000** ($15,000 less than my target price; $10,000 from my bottom-line price)
My Counter #1	**$389,000**
Buyer Offer #2	**$370,000** ($10,000 less than my target price; $5,000 from my bottom-line)
My Counter #2	**$385,000**
Buyer Final Offer, Accepted	**$381,000** ($1,000 over my target price)

****

Non-Monetary Currency

As I have covered earlier, there are sometimes opportunities to negotiate prices on non-monetary terms. For instance, if you are planning on painting the house before the sale you could offer to accept a lower price to avoid this cost and effort. The buyer may value this offer greatly because then they can paint in their color choices, and they like the discount. As a seller including a non-monetary officer can save you time, money, and hassle, and a buyer can see both financial and aesthetic opportunity.

Have a garage full of tools and junk and scrap metal? Tell the potential buyer if they take care of the clean-up you will take $1,000 off the price. Consider opportunities such as these to create a win-win scenario for you and the buyer.

After you have accepted an offer, an inspection is usually done by the buyer's engineer. Keep in mind that if issues arise you can remediate them yourself or you can lower the price somewhat to accommodate the cost of the repairs. Buyers will often accept a price reduction rather than have you remediate something. These kinds of arrangements speed up the sales process and ensure the closing date happens sooner. They also help you avoid the back and forth that can arise if a contractor is brought in to remediate a problem.

****

A Personal Example

I had a property on the market that I had planned on replacing the windows before the sale. A buyer came along who loved the design of the current windows and asked if I would leave them in place and reduce the price by $3,000. I was happy to agree because the replacing the window would have cost more than $10,000 and would have delayed the sale.

That was a win-win for me and the buyer.

****

In Chapter 4, I talk about of the different types of sellers' motivations that might impact your decision on buying a property, such as that owner who wanted me to continue leasing to his long-time tenant for at another year. When selling your property, there might be similar considerations that can impact your sale of the property as well. For example:

1. When does the buyer want to close? Obviously, if you have decided you want to cash out, faster is usually better, but sometimes you may have to hold on to a property a few months longer for various reasons, such as accommodating a tenant who wants to stay another month or two before the new owner moves in. I prefer a buyer acting with urgency versus one who has time on their hands. Time tends to increase the odds that the deal will fall through. There is a well-known expression in sales: "Time kills." My view of best practices in this area is to get to contract as soon as possible, and close the transaction as soon as possible.

2. What percent of the purchase price is the buyer putting down? A higher down payment shows a more qualified buyer. (Of course, 100% cash is ideal, but such offers are exceptional and very rare.) On the other end of the spectrum, beware of the 5% down-payment customer. These buyers can consume as much as three months of your time in the purchase process and then fall out for failure to get a mortgage. This can be devastating in a selling cycle, potentially leaving you with a six- to nine-

month delay in your sale. I have sold properties to people putting 5% down, but in a competitive context I will take a 30% down-payment customer over a 5% down-payment customer even if doing so costs me a percentage point or two off the purchase price. A high down-payment customer is almost sure to close.

3. Who is the buyer? Can they afford to purchase your property? Search online and see what they do for a living, confirm that they are working or retired from a good-paying job, check their credit if you can, understand why they are buying, and their motivation on timing.

4. Are there other terms and conditions? The ideal buyer is paying cash, has no mortgage and/or inspection contingency (or they have completed the inspection). Beware of any other terms the buyer inserts into their offer. In most cases, you want a simple clean offer to sell your property.

Summary

1. Sell from a position of strength, not in a weak market and not when you urgently need the money. Plan ahead!

2. The majority of buyers want a property to be tenant-free soon after closing or to have tenants on a month-to-month lease at closing so the buyers have the option to retain the tenant if they want to.

3. Hire a realtor with a record of success selling properties, not just because they are a friend or because they list lots of properties.

4. Don't be penny wise and pound foolish – pay market rate or better commissions to your realtor.

5. Price your property closer to the high end in your area but not too high.

6. Define your target price, asking price, and bottom-line price to guide your decisions.

7. Evaluate the strength and quality of an offer, considering factors beyond just the offered price. One key element of strength is a high percentage down payment.

8. Sell high!

Chapter 13 – Take Care
Avoid mistakes to ensure success

Throughout this book I have made suggestions on how to avoid certain errors that I have made and how to be most effective in your real estate investing endeavors. I thought it might be helpful to provide a few additional areas of caution to help ensure your success:

1. There are always opportunities to purchase investment properties at lower than market prices, but sometimes there are hidden reasons that the lower price exists. A property may be a bargain for a reason, so be cautious. For example, I came across a ½ acre lot near my home for $250,000, much lower than the market price for similarly sized lots in this area. I looked into acquiring the property as I was interested in building a multi-family home. Early in the process, I asked the selling realtor (who would double-end the deal, see glossary, page TK), "why is this lot priced so low and why has it been sitting on the market for so long?" Her answer surprised me, and also caused me to walk away from the transaction. Apparently more than a decade earlier there had been a gas station across the street that had had a major leak. Clearly there was a risk of contamination of the area surrounding the station, including this lot. I was very happy I had that information prior to purchasing the property, instead of learning about it after I invested $450,000 building a multi-family home on the property! Other risks you may encounter include an undisclosed but near final decision for a development to be built next door, pending changes in zoning laws, or a noise issue, such as commuter trains nearby.
2. Avoid long-distance real estate ownership – instead invest locally. Trying to manage real estate from a distance is kind of like long-distance relationships: they are difficult to manage and generally do not end well. The benefits of investing locally include the ability to leverage your own local knowledge of towns and streets and to get intimate with local realtors, and the physical availability to view, evaluate, and service properties that are reasonably close to you.
3. Beware of partnerships--they can be very tempting, especially early on, because real estate investments are expensive and

capital intensive. If you haven't yet made your first real estate profits, partnerships can help you get a head start. I have had the distinct advantage of being able to have my wife as my partner, and together we make an awesome team. However, there are times when even we disagree on when to buy or sell a property. Taking on partners that are not spouses creates all kinds of risk and you should think very carefully before entering into a partnership with a friend or, even more risky, a stranger. I am not saying do not do it under any circumstances, but I do suggest you be very cautious. Be sure to document the nature of the relationship, ownership percentages, and operating procedures. Build a responsibility matrix so it is clear who will be responsible for what, and determine in detail how all financials (expenses, income, and profits) will be divided. Do this even if it is a long-time friend you are investing with. Documenting everything will improve your odds of success, and will also ensure your friendship is not negatively affected by a lack of clarity in how the partnership is going to work.

4. Do not take on major construction projects early in your investment career, unless you are in the contracting business. We have discussed in Chapter 10 how you can optimize your assets through renovations, but it is not to take on a new and complex endeavor (real estate investing) and add to it the risk and complexity of a major construction project. Start with something simpler, a property that requires more moderate renovation, to gain experience and accumulate profits before taking on a large renovation.

5. Your credit rating is your life blood, watch after it with great care. You know your credit rating is important in matters such as obtaining a credit card, financing a car, or getting a mortgage, but to invest in real estate a high credit rating is absolutely crucial. Simply stated, if you can't borrow money to purchase properties, you can't succeed in this business. And if you have a weak credit rating but still can borrow, you are likely to have to pay two to three times the market rate, eating into or eliminating your profits. For all these reasons be hyper-vigilant about paying your bills on time to maintain a high credit rating.

6. Do not take on too many properties at once early on. You will stretch yourself financially and time wise. Pace yourself. Acquire a property, perhaps two, and learn as you go. Resist the temptation to do too much too fast.

7. Consider a property in "all seasons" before you buy it. If beauty and privacy is an important aspect in the value of a property you are considering, understand what that property will be like in all seasons. The warning here is to be aware if you are paying a higher price for privacy that you are certain that privacy exists year-round.

The best example is a property that in summer, with lush trees and leaves in the backyard creating great privacy, turns into a very not-private property once the leaves fall and the neighbors you didn't know existed are now very obtrusive. The above are considerations that could be important to your success so keep them in mind as you make your investment decisions!

Summary:

1. If a property is priced below market, understand why to ensure there are no underlying issues that damage future value.
2. Try to invest locally versus far from your day-to-day home.
3. Avoid complexity. Do this especially early on, including avoiding partners and keeping construction/renovation to a minimum in your first few investments.
4. Consider what the property would be like in all four seasons, not just what it is like in the season you are making the purchase.

Chapter 14 – Let's Go
On to profits

Congratulations! By reading to the end of this book, you have accelerated your real estate knowledge ahead by twenty years! It is my hope that you now feel inspired to proceed with your real estate investing endeavors armed with a great level of expertise. You have learned new methodologies that took me years to learn and have read Personal Examples of real-life situations that I have encountered during my investment experiences. Replicate the good ones, avoid the bad ones, and you will find success.

Before I let you go, let's review the Ideal Scenario once again, followed by my advice for your next actions.

The Ideal Scenario:
1. Buy Low! If you purchase your properties below market price you will have the security to know your assets have positive value immediately. Target 10% to 15% below market value for your purchase price. As a result, even before any appreciation you are ahead of the game.
2. Lease your property right away! Plan when you are in the process of acquiring a property and get that first tenant lined up to move in as close to your closing date as possible.
3. Find a great tenant! Check them out thoroughly, a relatively small amount of time will save you from much frustration and financial strain in the future.
4. Reduce your labor by putting much of the workload on your tenant.
5. Create positive cash flow! Ensure your lease rate is competitive and that it also covers your projected costs. Much of this analysis should be done as you are setting your target purchase price.
6. Finance your property with minimum costs! Procure a mortgage that keeps your monthly expenses to a minimum while protecting you from dramatic increased costs during your projected ownership period.
7. Keep that property occupied! When it is time for a new tenant, plan and line up that tenant for a move-in date within days of your existing tenant's departure.

8. Sell high! Get top dollar for your investment as you close out. You made money on the purchase, you made money while you owned the property, and now you will make money selling it.

What should you do now? Well, itis time for you to go out and get that first property! Turn the process described in this book into actions and reality.

Take your time on your first transaction. After all, you likely haven't had residential real estate in your investment portfolio up to now, so taking your time on the first one should not be an issue. While I'm not a fan of over-analyzing, on your first transaction gather lots of data, interact with realtors, study Craigslist, and get to know the pockets of investment real estate in your community. You want to apply the lessons you learned in this book, digest the data you gather from the sources I just described, and make a thoughtful acquisition in a low-stress timeframe.

Take your time. Make an unemotional decision. Set your target prices, stick to them, make and gain an accepted offer at or below your target price, and follow the Ideal Scenario from there.

After your first transaction, you will find yourself armed not only with the lessons of this book but also your own experiences. This makes you a much more powerful player going forward with high odds of success as you move to acquire other properties. Soon, thousands of dollars of profits will be yours. Then tens of thousands. And, eventually, hundreds of thousands! You can do it! You will do it! Good luck!

Appendix A: Financing Options

<u>Comparison of Loan Types*</u>
As you learned in Chapter 5, there are multiple financing options for real estate investors, and choosing the right one can have a major impact on your cash flow and profitability. In this section we will take a deep dive into three of the financing structures.

1. The 30-year fixed-rate mortgage. This is the most common, and most traditional, mortgage for homeowners and investors. Because it spreads out payments toward the principle over 30 years, the payments are lower than the 15-year mortgage even though the 15-year mortgage tends to have a lower interest rate.
2. The 15-year fixed rate mortgage. This is the second most common mortgage. It typically has a lower interest rate than the 30-year mortgage however since it is paid off in 15 years the monthly payments are higher than the 30-year mortgage.
3. The 30-year, 7/1 interest only adjustable rate mortgage. This type of mortgage is less common but it is one that I have used several times with great success.
   a. The 7 is the number of years during which the interest only provision applies. No principle is paid during the 7 years, resulting in a much lower monthly payment and minimizing your cash outflow during the time you own the property.
   b. The interest rate is also fixed during the first 7 years.

The 1 indicates the number of times the interest rate can be adjusted in any year from years 8 to 30. We will compare all three of these options in the tables below using an investment scenario with the following characteristics:

Property purchase price	**$250,000**
20% down payment	**$50,000**
Mortgage	**$200,000**
(Purchase price – down payment)	
Holding period, 7 years, then sell by the end of year 7	
Sales price	**$325,000**

*NOTE: I am not a certified financial advisor in any fashion and all information shared in this section is based on my experiences as an investor in real estate. You should consult your personal financial advisor for important financing decisions.

MORTGAGE COMPARISONS

Characteristics	30-Year Fixed	15-Year Fixed	7/1 Interest ARM
Total Number of Payments – Full Term	360	180	360
Total Payments Made this Scenario	84	84	84
Principle is Part of Payments	Yes	Yes	Yes
Interests is Part of Payments	Yes	Yes	Yes
Interest Rate this Scenario*	3.25 %	3.13 %	2.80 %
*Rates are examples based on 8/11/2020			

Conclusions Based on Key Data (See Table Next Pages)
1. The 7/1 interest only ARM option produces a significantly better cash flow with the monthly payment being almost half 30-Year Monthly Payment ($467 vs $871 vs $1,394, Row A).
2. The most profitable of the three financing options is the 30-year fixed-rate mortgage, but the profit is only approximately 2% more than the 7/1 mortgage.
3. The profit with all three financing options is within 5% of each other.
4. The 7/1 option defers payment of principle to the payout at the end of seven years. So, while you don't pay the principle during the loan period, you do have less equity in your home during the ownership period. This may or may not be meaningful to you depending on your financial situation and perspective on asset ownership.
5. See row D. Your interest expense is highest with the 30 year, lowest with the 15 year, and in between for the 7/1. $42,153, $35,235, and $39,228 respectively. These differences are accounted for in the total profit as shown in row K.

When I look at this data it is clear which mortgage structure I would choose for an asset I wanted to hold for three to seven years, and that is the 7/1 interest only ARM. This option minimizes my cash outflow and maximizes my positive cash flow over the life of the loan with minimal impact on my overall profit when I sell the property.

This is not to say that the 15- and 30-year options are "bad" choices. They each have their advantages. You may choose the 15- year mortgage because you can accept and manage the lower level of positive cash flow and feel more secure knowing you are paying down the principle in a more accelerated fashion. Said another way, you do this so you will "own" a higher portion of the property than you would otherwise.

The 30-year mortgage may appeal to someone who is more comfortable with a stable, long-term, more mainstream mortgage that allows for gradual reduction in principle during the ownership period.

Lastly, the 7/1 mortgage requires discipline and risk that the other two options do not. First, and very importantly, for the transaction as described in this section to be realized, the property MUST be sold by the end of year seven. If it is not, the remaining payments include an amortization of the full principle of the original loan ($200,000) over 23 years (due to the fact it is a 30-year mortgage, the first 7 years were interest only), AND the risk of an interest rate increase each year. For this reason, I recommend the 7/1 interest option only for someone who is certain their holding period will be seven years or less.

FINANCING OPTIONS; KEY DATA POINTS

		30-Year Fixed	15-Year Fixed	7/1 Interest ARM
A	Monthly Payments	$871	$1,394	$467
B	Total Annual Payments	$10,452	$16,728	$5,604
C	7-Year Total Payments	$73,164	$117,096	$39,228
D	Total Interest Paid	$42,153	$35,235	$39,228
E	Remaining Principle Due after 7 Years	$169,309	$118,205	$200,000
F	Sales Price after 7 Years	$325,000	$325,000	$325,000
G	Sales Price Less Principle Due	$155,961	$206,795	$125,000
H	Profit Without Rental Income	$32,847	$39,765	$35,772
I	Monthly Rental Income Less $500/Month Expense	$1,500	$1,500	$1,500
J	7 Year Total Rental Income Less $500 Expense	$126,000	$126,000	$126,000
K	Total Pre-Tax Profit	$158,847	$165,765	$161,772

NOTE: the above financial data is pre-tax. Please consult with your tax advisor to understand your actual results.

Glossary

ARM: Adjustable rate mortgage. This is a mortgage in which the interest rate can change during the term of the mortgage based on pre-defined rules and timeframes. There is usually a limit as to how much the interest rate can rise both annually and throughout the life of the mortgage (e.g. maximum annual increase of .5% per year, 3% maximum increase over the life of the loan).

Capitalization Rate (Cap Ra): A calculation used to help you determine what your Return on Investment (ROI) would be in an "all cash" scenario. The equation is *Net Operation Income + Purchase Price.*

Cash Sale: A cash sale is as it sounds, the buyer pays all cash and does not procure a mortgage. This is an ideal situation for a seller as the transaction can be quick and is likely to be completed by the buyer.

Comparables (aka Comps): These are properties similar to the one you are buying or selling. Comparable "sales" indicate actual values of recently sold homes. Comparable "listings" are properties that have not sold but may have market values to the one you are considering purchasing or selling. Comparable listings are a less reliable indicator that comparable sales.

Double-ended Deal: In the case of this real estate proposition, the sale and purchase involve only one agent instead of two. The agent who lists the property also sells the property, generating two commissions for the agent instead of splitting the commission between two agents. Example: Joe lists his home with Jane and her real estate firm. A buyer, John, contacts Jane and says he wants to purchase the property. On the sale of the property, Jane receives the selling and buying commissions (usually 5 or 6% of the selling price).

Equity: The part of the total value of your home that you own. Example: Your property has a real value of $250,000, and you have $150,000 of principle remaining on your mortgage, you have $100,000 of *equity*.

Instant Equity: The amount of equity generated when you purchase a property at below-market rates. Example: You purchase a property for $125,000 that you could sell within the next six months for $150,000. You gain $25,000 of *instant equity* on the purchase date.

Interest: The expense you pay the bank for allowing you to borrow the money to purchase your property.

Listing Agent: The real estate agent representing the seller of a property is the listing agent The listing agent and their firm are usually paid half the commission after the sale, often 2.5 or 3% of the selling price Example: If I want to sell a property from my portfolio, I would hire a listing agent to advertise it for me and represent me in interactions with potential and actual buyers.

Mortgage Contingency: When a seller and a buyer agree on the price for a property, they enter into a purchase contract. If the buyer needs to borrow money via a mortgage in order to complete the purchase, the contract is "contingent" on the buyer being able to gain approval for the mortgage.

Negative Equity: When you owe your mortgage provider more on than the value of your home. Example: You have a $200,000 mortgage and the home's market value is $175,000, you have $25,000 in *negative equity*.

Net Operating Income (NOI): A calculation used to help you (and your bank) determine the "operating revenue" on a property you own or are considering purchasing. The NOI also become a key input into calculating the Capitalization Rate (Cap Rate) and the Return on Investment (ROI). The equation is *Rental Income – Operating Expenses = NOI.*

Non-monetary Currency: Sometimes during a transaction for a property, you can trade something of value to a buyer or a seller that provides an incentive for them to close the transaction. For example, you could include an offer to perform certain upgrades, allow an existing tenant to stay after the sale/purchase, or extend timelines to close the transaction.

Plenty of Fish: This term is meant to encourage you not to get caught up in a single property you may want to purchase. If you cannot acquire a property at or below your target price, move on! There are plenty of fish in the sea (plenty of properties to invest in!).

Pre-renting: There is typically a lag time of 60-90 days after the sale of a property and before the transfer of a property is legally complete. During this time, the purchaser can "pre-rent," meaning they can list the property for rent the goal to have a new tenant move in immediately after the transfer is completed. The result is an immediate cash flow for the buyer of the property.

Principle: A mortgage typically has two components: principle and interest. The interest is the cost of the loan the principle is the equity portion of your payment. Example: Your mortgage payment is $1,000, $300 may go to principle and $700 to equity. After making the $1,000 payment you own $300 more of your home than you did previously, and the bank owns $300 less.

Return on Investment (ROI): A calculation used to determine the total return on your percentage gain on your investment in a real estate transaction (from start to finish, purchase through the ownership period until completion of sale). This is the most important calculation. The equation is *Gain on Investment – Cost of Investment ÷ Cost of Investment.*

Seller's Agent: The real estate agent representing a buyer looking for and/or making an offer on a property is the seller's agent. The seller's agent usually earns half the commission when their client purchases a property, often 2.5-3%. Example: If I want to purchase a property, I may hire a seller's agent to help me find a property that meets the characteristics I am looking for. Once you become an experienced real estate investor you can choose to contact a listing agent directly in order to leverage the incentive of a double-ended deal.

Target Price: The price that you set that you will not exceed in when negotiating for the purchase of a property. All of your offers will be at or below this price, and if your offers are not met you will move on to another property. Example: You set a *target price* of $200,000 for a property listed at $225,000; the seller will not accept an offer below $210,000; You walk away.

About the Author

Dan Papes had been successfully investing in residential real estate for more than 20 years. With each transaction and ownership experience, Dan's profits accumulated into the millions of dollars. Partnering with his energetic and insightful wife, Christina, he has purchased and sold more than 20 properties with only one unprofitable experience. With every property, every renovation, and every landlord/tenant experience, he learned new and better ways of executing in the market. This book is an aggregation of all that experience, now available to all who read it. His objective is to share his knowledge so that you can accelerate your success in your real estate career, essentially rocketing readers ahead 20 years in their experience.

For his "day job", he is an executive in the technology industry and has held the positions of President, Chief Revenue Officer, and Executive Vice President of Global Sales and Marketing. During his career (which is still active), his organizations generated more than $50 billion in revenue.

In 1998, Dan was a busy, young executive at IBM when he had a fateful Starbucks conversation with a close friend. That friend shared that he had recently begun construction on a multi-family home in a nearby community, and Dan pressed him with many questions about this new venture. What the friend told Dan convinced him to enter the residential real estate investment market. He began in earnest to learn all he could about such investments, and soon after purchased his first property. That purchase resulted in a six-figure profit in just two years. From that point, he was off and running in the real estate business, all while continuing his successful career in technology industry leadership roles.

Dan was born and raised in Westchester County, north of New York City and, after moving more than six times during his IBM career, he settled again with his family in Westchester. He and Christina have four children and are very active in their community. Dan has a Bachelor of Arts degree from Vanderbilt University.

Have questions? Get in touch with the author at:

dan@letsgetrealestate.org / @papesdaniel / https://www.letsgetrealestate.org

Acknowledgements

This book contains my accumulated knowledge from real estate investing over the last 20 years, but 16 years of those have been with my wife and partner, Christina Papes. Together we have bought, renovated, rented, and sold properties in New York and Florida. Without her, I would be far less successful. I am grateful for her no-nonsense approach to negotiations and her masterful ability to tastefully renovate properties with values ranging from $200,000 to $3 million. Most of all, this real estate journey would have been one-quarter the fun had it not been for her.

I would also like to acknowledge my childhood and life-long friend Jeff Burdick for introducing me to investing in residential real estate. It is Jeff who is referenced in the book at the point where I mention a fateful day in Starbucks when I became inspired by Jeff to invest as he had been doing. My editor, Alice Siempelkamp, who was introduced to me by my cousin and fellow author, Geoff Loftus. Her patience with my busy schedule, her encouragement, and professional input were invaluable. She also managed most of the logistics that enabled this book to be published. My thanks to my oldest son, Teddy, who created the fitting title for this book. Knowing that I wanted the book to be about actual experiences, not theories, he developed the apt title. And, lastly, Allie DeMartino, my graphics artist, who has done high quality work for me in both my personal and professional life. I sincerely hope that this team effort has resulted in a book that you will enjoy and learn from, and that will become the foundation for your success in real estate investing.